AMAZING LOVE

A LOOK AT

SONG OF SOLOMON

A LOVE LETTER FROM THE HEART OF GOD

BY
ROBERT LEX

A video is on Youtube
The Amazing Love of God Bob Lex

A PERSONAL NOTE

This book was written to help you come into an intimate relationship with Jesus. But before reading it there is something you need to know. All of us were born in sin. God decreed that the just penalty for sin is death — eternal separation from God. But in His love for us, for you, He placed this penalty upon His only son, Jesus Christ. He died for your sins and rose from the grave to make you right with God, filling you with God's goodness. You can receive this gift from God simply by asking for it. Jesus said, “Whoever desires let them come and take the water of life freely”.

I say this for 2 reasons: If you do not have a relationship with Jesus as your Saviour and Lord of your life then take this opportunity to do so. And this relationship with Jesus is necessary in order to be able to grasp the intimate depth of His love for you that is presented in this book. God created you for an intimate relationship with Himself. He did this because He wanted to. You are His special treasure and precious friend. There is a secret place with Jesus reserved just for you.

Bob

He is altogether lovely.

In this book is a revelation of the deep, passionate love of Jesus for you, personally.

AMAZING LOVE

A LOOK AT

SONG OF SOLOMON

A LOVE LETTER FROM THE HEART OF GOD

BY
ROBERT LEX

A Christian Voice Publishing

ISBN: 1934327042

Cover Design:
Nancy Scherer

Published by
A Christian Voice Publishing-Suite 202
2024 W. Superior St.
Duluth, MN 55806

The words of the songs used in this book are from the following songs:

Oh Lord, You're Beautiful by Keith Green.
Holy and Anointed One by John Barnett
Dance With Me by Chris Dupre
I Love You Lord by Laurie Klein
In The Garden by C. Austin Miles
Like Honey by Michael Brymer & Mark Ham

COMMENTS/ACKNOWLEDGEMENTS

There are many authors and individuals who have helped my journey of many years to a beginning understanding of the amazing love of God as so vividly expressed in Song of Solomon. I say, beginning understanding, because His love is too deep for me to fully grasp, at least while here on this Earth.

I believe this book, Amazing Love, has been inspired by Jesus Christ, and it is He who brings the revelation. But I wish to thank those who have allowed the Holy Spirit to speak through them. Some of the authors who over the years have contributed much are Tommy Tenney, Mike Bickle, Bob Sorge, John Piper, Phillip Keller. This is certainly not a complete list. But I submit these names that you, the reader, may find other sources to help lead you to that secret place with our Beloved Jesus.

I give special thanks to those who have given of their time to encourage me and make this become a reality.

I thank my wife, Carol, for the encouragement and the hours of typing and editing.

I thank Don Hanson with whom I collaborated, and who first encouraged me to go-for-it and publish it. And I thank Bob and Barb Demuth for their encouragement and advice; Lee Ann O'Hara, and Pastors Tom Porta and Mark Radeke for their encouragement.

I thank Steve Baker and Donna Falconer for their valuable help with the computer. And Karla Neumann for help with the songs.

AMAZING LOVE

A special thanks goes to Nancy Scherer for the inspired design and painting of the cover.

As explained in the Introduction, as God put this on my heart, it was not intended to be published but to be presented verbally to effect an impartation of His passionate love; to allow a soaking time enhanced by singing the referenced songs. But by the urging of others I decided to make the book public. Although not as effective as a verbal presentation, I trust the Holy Spirit will still use it to satisfy the longing soul. And I do intend to present it verbally as the Lord leads.

This book is for both unbelievers and believers. For unbelievers that through the revelation of God's love for them they will call upon the Lord Jesus and receive His gift of forgiveness and sweet fellowship now and for eternity. For both, my desire is that this book will lead you to an intimate relationship with the lover of your soul.

AMAZING LOVE

INTRODUCTION

This is an illumination on the book in the Bible titled Song of Solomon. Yes, King Solomon transcribed it, but it is not his. Jesus, the Son of God, is the author.

This is a love letter not from Solomon, but from the heart of God. This book reveals to us a God who is an affectionate Bridegroom overcome with passionate love for His bride. Jesus is the Bridegroom. All who desire Him are the bride, corporately as the church and individually. Song of Solomon is presented in terms of the love affair between a bride and her Bridegroom. Between you, the bride, and Jesus the Bridegroom.

Our relationship with God is to be a romance. Song of Solomon speaks to that through the eyes of a lovesick bride and lovesick Bridegroom.

Hosea in 2:16 long ago said, "**And it shall be in that day, says the Lord, that you will call Me, "my Husband" and no longer call Me "my Master."**

Song of Solomon puts into poetic words the burning love of the Father God for His children. Solomon wrote 1005 songs, but this is the chief of all the songs. It is a pastoral drama of singular loveliness. It is called the Song of Songs in the same manner that the most holy place in the tabernacle is called the Holy of Holies. A Rabbi, after saying, "All the books of the old testament are holy," described the Song of Songs as the holy of holies.

Song of Solomon is given to us in allegorical style because it reveals a love so deep, infinite, and so intense that mere words fail.

We must receive it as a Spirit to spirit revelation and impartation from the author of love, from the One who is love.

God often speaks of deep things in hidden language so that the spiritually hungry will seek out deeper meaning. Song of Solomon is a love song, therefore it is written in the poetic language of love, providing endless depths to enjoy. We need to read it visually, allowing the symbols and imagery to evoke a spiritual understanding, a feeling, knowing, sensing what it is intending to impart to us. It will draw word pictures for us.

In allegorical form, the King or Beloved is the true representation of Jesus the Bridegroom. The Shulammite is the type of the true believer. The Daughters of Jerusalem may be seekers not yet established in Christ. They are her virgin friends.

Song of Solomon is addressed to those who desire and long for a fuller experience of Jesus, an intimacy with Him as in Psalm 42, "**As a deer pants for water brooks so pants my soul for You, O God**." The purpose in this book is for this beautiful love song to bring us to a place of desire for Jesus, and at the same time satisfy that desire and bring us into a place of intimacy with Him

"Eat friends, and drink; drink deeply My beloved ones." (Song of Solomon 5:1) Yes, the desired outcome is that you will drink deeply.

This is not intended to be a study of the details, or a critical analysis of every word and phrase, but only as their deeper meanings impart to us the passionate love of the Lord reflected in them. The aim is for this book to speak its message of the passion of the Bridegroom for we the bride and in turn release that passion back to the Bridegroom, Jesus.

AMAZING LOVE

One can look at Song of Solomon in a number of ways, such as do's and don'ts. But here we will look at it in terms of "Be" to lead us into an intimate fellowship with Jesus. Jesus said, "If you love Me you will keep My commandments." Obedience is certainly vital to our relationship with Jesus. But from our love relationship the obedience part will flow and not become a burden or legalism or false.

The expressions of Song of Solomon are chaste, pure, romantic, delicate, sensuous, and always mysterious. They can be understood only with the heart. We must look at this book as a parable of divine love if we are to see under this earthly story a deep and holy, heavenly meaning.

We must take Song of Solomon as a precious love letter as from a sweetheart Take it to a secluded, secret place, sit and allow every passionate expression of the Bridegroom to flood your very being, and to in-turn pour out your love to Him, echoing the words of the Shulamite, with expressions from your own heart.

Song of Solomon sounds to those who have eaten it and experienced it like the far off echoes of the new song, which only the redeemed from the earth could learn. What could be sweeter than, "I am my Beloved's and He is mine," which is repeated three times in Song of Solomon.

Like the fragrance and beauty of a lovely flower, the beauty of Jesus cannot be described. It must be experienced.

"Eat, O friends, and drink; drink deeply, My beloved ones."
God's love is altogether wonderful, beyond our comprehension, and entirely inexhaustible in its scope and intensity.

To know and experience the full love of Christ is the happy and eternal pursuit of all lovers of God. This therefore is the purpose of this commentary to usher us in, to know and experience the width, length, height and depth of the love of the "Beautiful One," Jesus.

Isaiah 55:1, **"Ho, everyone who thirsts, come to the waters. And you, who have no money, come, buy and eat. Yes come, buy wine and milk without money and without price."**

The agenda is that you, the bride of Christ, might be set ablaze with an exclusive and fiery passion for your Bridegroom, your Beloved Jesus. How will you accomplish this?

Jeremiah declared in 15:16, "**Your words were found and I ate them, and Your Word was to me the joy and rejoicing of my heart."**

This book,Amazing Love, is written for whosoever will." Jesus said in John 6:47, "**Most assuredly I say to you that whosoever believes in Me has eternal life."**

Jesus desires an intimate relationship with you. He is brooding over you, gently calling you into oneness with Himself.

Before you journey through Song of Solomon, during your journey, or after, if you are hungry for a relationship, an intimacy with the Lover of your soul, just make it known to Him. **"Whosoever calls upon the name of Christ Jesus will be saved" (Romans 10:13). "Whosoever desires let them take the water of life freely**" (Revelation 22:17).

First read Song of Solomon. Just read it even though you probably will not understand much, or any of it. Then go back and "eat the words" using this commentary to guide you through it. Cherish it and absorb it into your very being as you would a passionate love letter from your earthly sweetheart. Keep the focus in mind that Song of Solomon is a personal love letter to you.

This book is based on the New King James version of the Bible because I believe it is the closest to the poetic, allegorical style of its Eastern origin.

Eat O' friends and drink, drink deeply O, beloved ones.

CHAPTER 1

Verses 1-4 - **"Let Him kiss me with the kisses of His mouth. For Your love is better than wine. Because of the fragrance of Your good ointments, Your name is ointment poured forth. Therefore, the virgins love You. Lead me away. We will run after You. The King has brought me into His chambers. We will rejoice in You. We will remember Your love more than wine".**

This can be looked at as a chorus blending of the voice of the Shulamite with her friends.

This phrase is symbolic of the touch of the Word upon the human heart. It is a kiss better than any other, the reality of which a human kiss is merely a dim reflection.

Another version portrays the thoughts in these verses in a contemporary way to help our heart revelation. **"Kiss me again and again for Your love is sweeter than wine. Because of the fragrance of Your good ointments, Your name is ointment poured forth. No wonder all the young girls love You. Take me with You, come let's run. Lovely and delightful are You."**

There was a woman who got hold of that (Luke 7:36-39). **"One of the Pharisees asked Jesus to eat with him and Jesus went to his house and sat down to eat. And then a woman in the city, who was a sinner, when she knew that Jesus sat at the table in the Pharisees' house, brought an alabaster flask of fragrant oil and stood at His feet behind Him weeping. And she washed His feet with her tears and wiped them with the hair of her head. And she kissed His feet and anointed them with the fragrant oil."** A woman of the street, she brought a flask of fragrant oil and weeping she washed His feet with her tears, wiped them with her hair, kissed His feet and anointed them with the expensive oil. This was a prostitute who found the passionate love of Jesus.

"Rich Thy perfumes, but richer far than they the countless charms that round Thy person play. Thy name alone, more fragrant than the rose, glads every maid, where're its fragrance flows."

Orientals have always been passionately fond of perfumes. Even today the nomad ladies make treasure of any perfume they have.

His kiss is the assurance of pardon filling us with peace, joy, hope, and as well as the thrill of it, the intoxication, exhilaration, breathlessness, ecstasy. The sweetness of His lips is such that just one kiss would be eternal rapture.

We have to use words to communicate, but none are adequate. They only help us to feel in our spirit, and even our soul. God uses words in the Bible, but the words must impart their truth as we "eat" them.

To make perfume from a rose it must be crushed. To enjoy the fragrance in a flask it has to be poured out. Jesus was broken and crushed so that we might enjoy the fragrance and others enjoy His fragrance through us. "Your name is ointment poured forth."

II Corinthians 2:15 – **"For we are the sweet fragrance of Christ unto God, discernable to those who are being saved and also to those who are perishing."** The wonderful truth here is that the fragrance of Jesus, that ointment poured forth from Him, is also flowing from each of us who are His.

The Christian soul longs for the enjoyment of the Savior's love. We can express the phrase, "The Son of God loves me and gave Himself for me", but yet still long for the fullness of the blessed love. "The love of Jesus, what is it, none but His loved ones know it."

Psalm 63 – **"O God, You are my God; early will I seek You. My soul thirsts for You, my flesh longs for You in a dry and thirsty land where there is no water."**

Psalm 42 – **"As a deer pants for the water brooks, so pants my soul for You, O God. My soul thirsts for God, for the living God. When shall I come and appear before God."**

Revelations 3:20 – **" Behold, I stand at the door and knock. If you hear My knock and open the door I will come in and have sweet fellowship with you."**

Jeremiah 31:3 – **"The Lord appeared to me saying, I have loved you with an everlasting love, therefore with loving kindness I have drawn you."**

And with great joy we respond, "Lead me away, take me with You, come let's run."

Try to feel this, imagine it, allow it to draw a picture and impart to you what it is really portraying. This can be very vivid to young lovers. Picture this. A young couple much in love, engaged to be married. After an absence of a few days they meet. As her lover approaches, she runs and throws herself on him with total abandon, with no thought of anything but her bridegroom. She clutches him and cries out, "I want to be with you always, take me with you, come on let's run."

The daughters of Jerusalem get caught up in this with the Shulamite. They share in the brides rejoicing, declaring, "We will run after You, Jesus, we will be glad and rejoice in You, we will remember Your love more than wine." And the Shulamite confirms their sentiments with, "Rightly do they love You." It is as if she is shouting, "Oh yes, yes how could they not love Him."

These thoughts close with a bold, startling statement; "The king has brought me into His chambers." This is referring to Jesus, our Bridegroom, our King bringing the believer, the one who says, "take me with You, come lets run", into His chamber, into His secret place. Psalm 91 says, **"He who abides in the secret place of the most high shall abide under the shadow of the Almighty."** This marks the beginning of an intimate communion with the bride and special revelation of Himself to her.

Psalm 45 is called a psalm of the great king. Verse 13 is exceptionally beautiful, **"The royal daughter is all glorious within the palace, her clothing is woven with gold. She shall be brought to the king in robes of many colors. The virgins, her companions who follow her shall be brought to You. With gladness and rejoicing they shall be brought. They shall enter the king's palace."**

Verses 5,6 –**"I am dark (black) but lovely."** She acknowledges herself to be a country girl. She has been living in the fields and is browned with the ruddy health of a country life.

By her own confession she was tanned, (sun burnt) black, swarthy from tending the vineyards of her brothers. Then, and even yet, women were treated poorly in the East. Her brothers would have little compassion for her. She had no time to tend her own vineyard.

She is black as the tents of wandering Arabs but comely as the magnificent curtains in the palaces of Solomon. The believer is black, as being defiled and sinful by nature, but comely, as renewed by Divine grace to the holy image of God, accepted by Christ. This is a Cinderella analogy. We were the wretched slaves of sin, in toil and sorrow, weary and heavy laden, under a cruel taskmaster, but then a Prince – the Prince of Peace, rescues us.

The bride, the Lamb's betrothed, sees the beauty of the Lord reflected in herself and rejoices in her own attractions for His sake. His beauty is reflected in you also.

Verses 7,8 - **"Tell me O You whom I love where You feed Your flock, where You make it rest at noon. For why should I be as one who veils herself by the flocks of Your companions? If you do not know, O fairest among women, follow in the footsteps of the flock, and feed your little goats beside the shepherds tents."**

In running to her lover she would spend the siesta hour with Him. If she could not find Him she would have to wander aimlessly beside the other shepherds in whom she took no interest.

The soul, which longs for the enjoyment of fellowship with God, desires to be carried away out of all distractions, out of all restraints, lifted above reserve and above doubt into the closest and most loving union.

"If you do not know." Those who would be lifted up into the highest enjoyments of the Lord must not be impatient and doubt that He will reveal Himself. They must go quietly and patiently on with life, "in the footsteps of the flock."

John 1: 35-39 – As John the Baptist stood with Peter and Andrew, Jesus walked by and John said, **"Behold the Lamb of God."** Peter and Andrew heard this, turned after Jesus who said, **"What do you seek?"** They said, **"Rabbi, where are You staying?"** In other words, **"May we come with You?"** Jesus answered their heart cry, **"Come and see."**

As the Shulamite cries out, "Where do You feed your flock?" ("Where are You Staying?") The Bridegroom replies, "Come and see." Jesus' love letter of invitation, as the Bridegroom in Song of Solomon, becomes reality in Peter and Andrew. His desire from before time for intimate relationship with us becomes reality in these two as He invites them, "come and see."

From Verse 1-4 it is clear that her desire is not just in passing but is a deep longing to feast upon His beauty. There is no reason that she should remain veiled in His presence. In 2:14 Jesus expresses His desire to see her face unveiled. **"O my dove let Me see your countenance."** Could these verses be the first invitation from the Bridegroom to a place of intimacy?

Verse 9 - **"I have compared you My love to My filly among Pharaoh's chariots."**

In the East a beautiful mare was highly prized. In Damascus the mare comes before wife and child. The mare may be worth thousands of dollars and there is no more beautiful creature. The Egyptian horse was once prized as the Arab horse is now. The idea is that of stately beauty and graceful movements.

Verses 10,11 - **"Your cheeks are lovely with ornaments, your neck with chains of gold. We will make you ornaments of gold with studs of silver."**

Ezekiel 16 is God's declaration of his mercy and love for Israel, and their rejection of it. But for our purposes to see the analogy to Song of Solomon 1:10, feel God's heart in Ezekiel 16: 9-14.

"Then I washed you in water, yes I thoroughly washed off your blood, and I anointed you with oil. I clothed you in embroidered cloth, and gave you sandals of badger skin. I clothed you with fine linen and covered you with silk. I

adorned you with ornaments, put bracelets on your wrists, and a chain on your neck. And I put a jewel in your nose, earrings in your ears, and a beautiful crown on your head. Thus you were adorned with gold and silver, and your clothing was of fine linen, silk and embroidered cloth. You ate pastry of fine flour, honey, and oil. You were exceedingly beautiful, and succeeded to royalty. Your fame went out among the nations because of your beauty, for it was perfect through My splendor which I had bestowed upon you."

In these verses 1:9 through 2:3 we feast upon a beautiful picture of the love language exchanged between the bride and Bridegroom. This of course is a picture of Jesus and His bride, Jesus and you.

In His wisdom and foresight, Jesus sees us (Shulamite) as we will be when His love for us has completed its work. He relates to us on that basis. And so He invites her to a place of nearness, fellowship, and friendship, the banqueting house, and sustains her with expression of His deepest affection.

The Bridegroom is giving high praises to His bride, and it appears that the Daughters have caught the excitement and also want to honor the bride with ornaments. As seen in Ezekiel 16, God Himself gave gifts of jewelry to His loved ones. Jewelry was not something to be despised. It made them physically beautiful. I believe it was an outward expression of the inward beauty bestowed by God. And I believe that the jewelry is a type of the inner beauty, the spiritual beauty bestowed by the Bridegroom on His bride. Perhaps the jewelry we wear can be a visible reminder to us of how beautiful we are to our Bridegroom.

But as we see in Ezekiel 16:15, the Israelites began to trust in their own beauty, causing God to withdraw His beauty from them**." But you trusted in your own beauty, played the harlot because of your fame, and poured out your harlotry on everyone passing**

by who would have it." Many dimensions of Jesus' beauty and our beauty are linked to the revelations in Song of Solomon.

There is pain in his love, for in Matthew 23:37 Jerusalem, representing the bride, refuses His invitation and His passionate heart is broken as He longs for the love of His bride. **"O Jerusalem, Jerusalem, the one who kills the prophets and stones those who are sent to her. How often I wanted to gather your children together as a hen gathers her chicks under her wings but you were not willing."**

JESUS THE BRIDEGROOM DESIRES US. Our Bridegroom has indescribable desire for us and delight in us. It is in Him that we feel liked, enjoyed, wanted, pursued, and delighted. And something resonates in us when we grasp the burning desire of God's heart. Something profound happens in us when even in our weakness and brokenness we feel wanted, longed for, and rejoiced over. Our response then would be to abandon our hearts to God. When we can see Jesus as our Bridegroom, our need to feel enjoyed by God is met. The revelation of the Bridegroom was preached by Paul in 2 Cor. 11:2, **"For I am jealous for you with godly jealousy. For I have betrothed you to one husband that I may present you as a chaste virgin to Christ."**

NOTE: Both the Father and the Bridegroom desire us. Isaiah 62:5b, **"As a bridegroom rejoices over the bride, so shall your God rejoice over you."**

HE HAS PLANS FOR US. The Bridegroom has plans to share intimacy and power with us. Revelation 3:21 – **"To him who overcomes I will grant to sit with Me on My throne, as I also overcame and sat down with My Father on His throne."**

We have married an indescribably rich Bridegroom, into the aristocracy of the eternal city. Developing our relationship with the Bridegroom is the best way we will come to know the fullness of His plan for us.

PRAYER

I will draw near to you, Jesus. You are my life and my joy. Thank You for inviting me to come and see. My heart burns to know You more, and my longing is that I might find You and hear Your voice more clearly. Kiss me again, Lord, with the kisses of your mouth, and cause me to know the truth of Your love for me.

This song expresses our love for our Bridegroom, Jesus.

LIKE HONEY
You have stolen away my heart
With one glance of Your eye
How much more pleasing is Your love than choicest wine

Altogether lovely
You are wonderful and true
Let me hear You call my name
Draw me after You!

Like Honey on my lips –is Your name, O Lord!
(repeat)

O lover of my heart
You are my one desire
Your love as strong as death
Consume me with its fire

Many waters cannot quench
Nor rivers wash away
Your jealous love
Unyielding as the grave

Verses 12-15 - **"While the king is at His table, my spikenard sends forth its fragrance. A bundle of myrrh is my beloved to me that lies all night between my breasts. My beloved is to me a cluster of henna blooms in the vineyards of En Gedi."**

En Gedi is an oasis, a most delightful place on the west shore of the Dead Sea, an oasis of luxurious vegetation. The henna is a fragrant yellow white flower that grows in clusters like grapes, and is still found at En Gedi.

A song expresses the sentiment of verses 12-14, which may still be popular in the Middle East.

Make of me a silver necklace, and toss me about on Thy breast.
Make of me a golden earring, and hang me in Thine ear.

Having been invited to the place of intimacy (V8) she begins to express the romantic inclinations of her heart by declaring that her perfume is drawing His attention, even as He sits at the dinner table. In Verses 13, 14 then she expresses the passions of her heart giving poetic expression to that which burns inside.

"A bundle of myrrh is my Beloved to me that lies all night between my breasts." Some of the characteristics of myrrh are:

1. An embalming spice which was used to embalm Jesus.
2. A preservative. It keeps things from corrupting, putrefying, and rotting.
3. A beautifying quality. It is good to take away wrinkles from the face and make the skin smooth and shining.
4. The first principle ingredient of the holy anointing oil that was appointed to be used for the anointing of Aaron and the tabernacle.
5. Has a healing quality.
6. Is a perfume. Women wore little flasks of myrrh on their breast.

In Chapter 1:4 the Shulamite declares, **"Lead me away. I will follow You."** This is a total commitment. Come let us run together. To her joy then she clutches this precious myrrh close to her heart. This represents to us that this myrrh is the very essence, the life of Jesus filling us. This life begins to preserve us from corruption, to beautify us removing all spots and blemishes. Ephesians 5:27 - **"He will present the church (bride) to Himself, a glorious bride not having spot or wrinkle or any such thing, but that it should be holy and without blemish."** It has brought an anointing upon her that has begun to break the yoke of bondage. It has begun to heal. It has produced a fragrance within her such that she has become the fragrance of Christ in every place.

The bundle of Myrrh which is the beloved Jesus to us brings an anointing that breaks the yoke of bondage. It heals. Its fragrance becomes our fragrance.

There is something inside us (placed there by God) that will not be satisfied until we are able to release our love in a fervent single-mindedness that brings focus and passion to everything we do. The awareness of this longing causes an ache in our soul that simply cannot be satisfied except by the touch of the infinite Lover, and by our response of commitment to Him.

Verse 15 – **"Behold you are fair my love. Behold you are fair. You have dove's eyes."** The king responds, articulating the very thing she longs to hear – his fiery words instilling in her heart a passion deeper than she has ever known. **"You are fair My love."** You are beautiful to look upon.

"You have doves eyes." He is declaring to her that in His view she, although still immature, has already reached the single-minded fervency of love that her heart desires. A dove has tunnel vision. We could paraphrase this as; **"you have tunnel vision for Me only, and are not distracted with other affections and desires."**

Verses 16,17 and Chapter 2 Verse 1 - **"Behold, You are handsome my Beloved, yes, pleasant. Also, our bed is green. The beams of our houses are cedar, and our rafters of fir (cypress). I am the rose of Sharon and lily of the valley."**

Green = freshness, invigorating, flourishing. In the Hebrew language the word green is very suggestive. It is said to combine in itself the ideas of softness and juicy freshness, perhaps also of bending and elasticity.
Cedar = a noble and stately tree, it mounts high toward heaven, has deep roots, its shadow is refreshing, many birds dwell under it,and it was used to build Solomon's' temple.
Cypress = also used in building Solomon's temple. The Aramaic word is "our pleasant retreat is cypresses, beautiful and fragrant."

Psalm 92:12-15 – **"The righteous shall flourish like a palm tree. They shall grow like a cedar in Lebanon. Those who are planted in the house of the Lord shall flourish in the courts of our God. They shall still bear fruit in old age; they shall be fresh and flourishing (green) to declare that the Lord is upright. He is our rock and there is no unrighteousness in Him."**

There are different renderings of these verses. The Shulamite was a country girl. As she said in Verse 17, she was a rose of Sharon and lily of the valley. Her beauty is the beauty of nature, artless and pure. So we take this description as being not of a palatial splendor but of a sweet country home, a refreshing resting place. Her words could be, "My home is a soft, refreshing home, take me there my Beloved."

Again she is saying in effect, "I am a tender maiden who was brought up in a simple life, take me to a natural palace, to the green fragrant surroundings where the meadow flower, the valley-lily, will be happy."

So in light of our objective to glean from Song of Solomon the affectionate love affair between the bride and Bridegroom, between Jesus and each of us, how can we grasp what these two verses are trying to impart to us, to plant within us. In Revelation, Heaven is presented as a place of unimaginable splendor, golden streets, gates of pearls, crowns, and the throne. Solomon's temple is but a dim reflection of the eternal temple.

Song of Solomon refers more to gardens than palaces. Even in chapter 2 the words used are apples, fruit, gazelles, doves, green figs, tender grapes, etc.

Why is most of this book of Solomon presented in a pastoral setting? It shows a delight in the beauties of nature such as we might look for in Him who spoke of trees, from the cedar in Lebanon even to the hyssop that springs out of the wall. He spoke of beasts and fowl, of creeping things.

CHAPTER 2

Verse 2 - The Bridegroom will not allow His bride to depreciate her own value. **"Like a lily among thorns, so is My love among the daughters."** The king takes up the words of the bride. She is to Him as a lily. Other maidens, when compared to her, are but as thorns. There are tares in the Lord's field, barren fig trees in His garden. The thorns set forth by contrast the beauty of the lily.

The church, Christ's beautiful lily, will be changed into His likeness and reign with Him. The thing to grasp here is that the Lord looks at us even now as being this lovely lily. We need to see ourselves through His eyes.
A lily is a very sweet flower, so fragrant that a person's senses will be easily tuned with the strength of its fragrance. A lily is an exceedingly white flower. There is nothing more pure, nothing whiter.

The lily is a flower most gloriously adorned and lovely to look upon. Jesus said, "Solomon in all his glory was not arrayed like these." Its form is excellent. It has six white leaves, within are seven grains, and all within is the glory of gold. It hangs down its head. Much of the glory of the lily is inward. The bride is as the lily, glorious and delicate.

Verse 3- **"Like an apple tree among the trees of the woods, so is my Beloved among the sons. I sat down in the shade with great delight, and His fruit was sweet to my taste."**

The bride likens Jesus, the Bridegroom, to the beautiful, flowering fruit bearing apple tree. It gives welcome shade, its fruit gratifies the sense of taste, and to the Orientals is a symbol of love. She sat down under the shade of this tree, which, of course, is a position of rest, trust, and relaxing in the security of God.

Psalm 91:1 – **"He who dwells in the secret place of the Most High shall abide under the shadow of the Almighty."**

Dwell = sit down and be still, live there
Secret Place = one meaning is a covert, a hiding place
Shadow = a shelter that a mother bird gives her brood.

In the spring the beauty of the flowering apple tree, and the perfume of its blossoms is something that cannot be adequately described by words. It must be felt within the soul. Just as Jesus' loveliness and fragrance can be compared to the apple tree in bloom we must experience Him to know Him. I believe this example, and in reality the whole of Song of Solomon, is describing Him and His passion for His bride, but the words are only an invitation to "taste and see."

Try to describe a beautiful sunset to someone, or the taste of a sweet orange. You can only use expressions to stimulate one to try it, for them to taste and see. Just as Jesus said in Revelation 3:21, **"I stand at the door and knock, but you have to open the door and allow Me to reveal Myself to you."**

The shadow under which the one finds rest must be the shadow of the cross. Jesus is to the believer, "A refuge from the storm, a shadow from the heat, the shadow of a great rock in a weary land." (Isaiah 24: 4, 32:2)

It is delight in the Savior's love, which draws us to the cross.

Verse 4 – **"He brought me into His banqueting house, and His banner over me is love."**

The banqueting house is the House of Wine. In the culture of the Middle East, the House of Wine was the style of the day. It is rooted in the most romantic tradition, the engagement feast given upon the public announcement of the betrothal of a man to his prospective bride. The House of Wine is the formal setting for the betrothal feast. Subsequent Banquets of Wine were given to rehearse and celebrate the romance and intimacy of the days of first love. During the Banquet of Wine the prospective groom would at some point fill a glass with wine and set it on a table in plain view. In so doing the groom was saying, "Here I am. This cup of wine represents everything I am and all that I own. I am pouring out my life for you at this moment as I propose marriage. Will you take me as your own?"

It was a vulnerable and poignant moment, for the heart of the groom was on display for all to see, exposed and unprotected. At some time later in the evening the bride was expected to approach the table and take the cup in her hand to make a response by drinking of it. By doing so she was saying, "Yes, I will have you. My life is now sustained by yours, and you and I are one."

There is a powerful connection to the Lord's Supper (Communion) given at Passover, a Banquet of Wine. The mingling of the symbols – the bread from the Passover meal, the cup of wine from the betrothal banquet was in fact the proposal of marriage from Jesus, the Eternal Bridegroom to His disciples, who stood as the mystical Bride of Christ.

Jesus was extending His heart to His people with all the vulnerability and exposure of a groom at the Banquet of Wine, and saying to us, "Will you have Me? I long to have you as Mine alone." When we come to the Lord's Supper, we are coming as in the House of Wine recalling to our minds, and to His, the romance and joy that drove Him to the cross on our behalf.

"He brought me to the banqueting house." This reminds us of the Lord's words in Matthew 26:29, **"I say to you, I will not drink henceforth of this fruit of the vine until the day when I drink it new with you in My Fathers' Kingdom."** Our Banqueting House is one not made with hands, eternal in the heavens.

"His banner over me is love." The royal banner, the standard that had often led the warriors of Israel to battle, signalized the Banqueting House of the King of Israel. But what drew the bride was the love of the Bridegroom. That was the banner, which was beautiful in her eyes, which was over her. The banner of the cross is over the followers of the Lord. The banner is the Lord himself – His presence, His passion for His bride. The love of Jesus for His bride is very personal.

Heart of man cannot tell what will be the joy of those who in the heavenly banqueting house will sit down at the marriage supper of the Lamb. Then the bride will be arrayed in fine linen, clean and white, the fine linen that is the righteousness of the saints.

Then each true soldier of the cross who with that banner floating over them, having fought the good fight of faith, will see that banner in all its glorious beauty, and sit beneath it very near the King Bridegroom.

Verse 5 – **"Sustain me with cakes of raisins, refresh me with apples, for I am lovesick."**

The joy of the Bridegroom's love is too great and overwhelming; she is fainting in delight too sweet for her to endure. She asks for a restorative; cakes of raisins and other fruits which are credited with reviving and strengthening powers.

Verse 6 – **"Oh that His left hand were under my head and His right hand would embrace me."**

Here the bride longs for even more tender tokens of affection. We long to be drawn ever closer into the Lord's embrace.

A song will help us draw closer to Jesus our Bridegroom.
"O Lord, you're beautiful, Your face is all I seek. And when Your eyes are on this child, your grace abounds to me."

Isaiah 40: 11 – **"He will feed His flock like a shepherd. He will gather the lambs with His arm and carry them in His bosom, and gently lead those who are with young."**

As His precious ones, His lambs, we are supported in those tender, those protecting arms when we must pass through trials, difficulties, tribulations, suffering.

Deuteronomy 33:27 – **"The eternal God is your refuge, and underneath are the everlasting arms ."**

Psalm 63: 8 – **"My soul clings to You. Your right hand upholds me."**

Verse 7 – **"I charge you, O daughters of Jerusalem by the gazelles or by the does of the field, do not stir up or awaken love until it pleases."**

The love between the Bridegroom and bride is true and pure. It is sacred and tender. Hence the use of gazelles or does who are gentle, timid creatures. The bride longs for the Bridegroom's love, but the daughters of Jerusalem must not try to excite it. It is more delicate, more maidenly, to wait till love pleases to stir itself, till it springs up spontaneously in the heart of the Beloved.

The relations of the soul with Christ are very sacred. They may be mentioned only to the like-minded and even then only with certain awe and reserve. And there are some communions of the heart with the heavenly Bridegroom which may be divulged to none, not even to the nearest and dearest.

And we must wait in patience for the Bridegroom. This is one of our most difficult times, for if for a time we cannot see Him or discern the tokens of His love, we must wait for His good time.

The love between the bride and the Bridegroom is sacred. The daughters of Jerusalem were to listen in silence. They were not to praise or to blame. They were not to endeavor to stimulate or increase the love of the bride or Bridegroom. They were to leave it to its free and spontaneous growth in the heart. It is not to be much talked of. It is to be treasured in the heart. It is that inmost spring of that life which is hidden with Christ in God. It must not be stirred by irreverent talk or disclosure, but it must rest unseen until it pleases – till the right time shall come for speaking of its blessedness.

Matthew 23:37 – **"O Jerusalem, Jerusalem."** Here the Lord's heart is filled with grief because the city, as the representation of His bride, has refused His invitation to intimacy. He is giving testimony to the passion burning in His heart; the same passion that caused Him to speak in such intimate terms over His dark but lovely bride. (Chapter 1:6)

PRAYER

Jesus, I will receive Your invitation to the place of intimacy in prayer. I long to hear Your voice telling me the truth of whom I am, and how You love me. I long to live out of the place of affirmation that comes from Your heart, and that liberates me to love You in return and live in the beauty of Your holiness. Draw me, Lord, and I will follow after You.

Verses 8,9 – **"The voice of my Beloved. Behold He comes leaping upon the mountains, skipping upon the hills. My Beloved is like a gazelle or a young stag. Behold He stands behind our wall. He is looking through the windows, gazing through the lattice."**

In these verses He surprises the Shulamite by appearing in an unexpected character, skipping upon the hills, leaping upon the mountains. This is a demonstration of the sovereign power of the Beloved over all the obstacles of life, the hills and mountains that seem to us unconquerable hindrances. In our parallel relationship with Jesus we have to confront a crucial question: Will we allow Him to draw us past the things that have regularly defeated us in our attempt to faithfully follow Him. "Lead me away and I will run after You."

Here we see that the King of Israel sought her in her humble home among the mountains of Lebanon. There He wooed and won her to be His bride. Just so the heavenly Bridegroom, the true Solomon who built the spiritual temple of living stones, came from His glorious throne to seek His bride, we, the church. And so He continues to come to seek and to save that which was lost.

The bride hears the voice of the Beloved. "My beloved" she says. In this little phrase, "My beloved", lies great depth. And this is the heart of our search for that depth in the Song of Solomon. If we come to that place of sincerity where we can declare, "My Savior, my Lord and my God, my King, my Beloved," then we can grasp the language of this holy Song of Songs, and see the spiritual meaning which underlies its touching parable of love.

We can look back with gratitude and joy to the days of our first meeting with Jesus, when we first heard the Saviors' voice calling us to Himself, when we first felt, He loves me.

The Beloved is seen bounding over the mountains, like a gazelle or young hart, fair to look upon and graceful. He stands by the wall of the humble cottage; He looks in through the window, through the lattice. There are spiritual meanings in these verses, and one of the feelings in this is the great excitement of the Bridegroom to see His bride. This is declared in Verse 14. **"O My dove, in the clefts of the rock, in the secret places of the cliff, let Me see your countenance, let Me hear your voice for your voice is sweet and your countenance is lovely."**

The emphasis is on His majesty, beauty and power, and ability to take the Shulamite with Him as He leaps and dances over the mountains in her life. He draws her after Him, reminding her that she is hidden in the cleft of a rock – a euphemism for the riven side of Christ. It is in this context that she is safe. "Mountain" symbolizes Kingdom. So the Lord here manifests His triumph over every power, leaping and skipping over the power of every foe with all things under His feet.

Psalm 3:3 – **"You, O Lord are a shield for me. My glory and the one who lifts up my head."** Jesus is known by the title, Tender Shepherd. He lifts your head when you are hurting and as you gaze into His compassionate eyes all the hurt melts away.

To regard the Lord as a gazelle or hart is similar to the title of Psalm 22, called "Aijeleth Hashshahar" or the hind of morning. Psalm 22 points toward the resurrection of Jesus. Just as morning is the beginning of the day, the resurrection of Christ is the beginning of new life. The hart is noted for its beauty and swiftness of escape from its enemies, and walks on the high places of the earth. So we see Jesus desiring for the maiden, His bride, to follow Him in all the beauty, victory and swiftness of His resurrection life.

Never is the church, His bride, we as individuals, forgotten or neglected. Never does He neglect or treat with indifference those for whom He died. 1) He makes himself acquainted with our needs. 2) He looks with affectionate kindness upon us who are dependent upon His favor. 3) His gracious regard awakens in us the desire to know Him more intimately. To see Him once is to wish to see Him again. Once we get a glimpse of His beauty and His affection for us, we are irresistibly drawn to Him.

Psalm 27 speaks to this. **"One thing have I desired of the Lord, that will I seek. That I may dwell in the house of the Lord all the days of my life, to behold the beauty of the Lord and to inquire in His temple**.

Verse 10- **"My Beloved spoke and said to me, "rise up My love My fair one and come away."**

"My fair one." Such a name of endearment tells the truth as to what we are to Him. Also in Verse 14, **"My dove."** What mother does not think her child is lovelier than everyone else's. Other people don't see it – she does. And so Christ sees in us what we cannot see. Back to Chapter 1:15, the Bridegroom declares, **"Behold you are fair My love, behold you are fair."** Beautiful to look upon.

"And come away." In Chapter 1 the bride proclaims, **"Lead me away, I will run after You."** Here now the Bridegroom responds and invites her to come away with Him. What a beautiful picture of two lovers so deeply in love. Jesus my beloved I hunger to walk with You, to go away with You. Yes My dove, come let us skip away together.

Verses 11-13- **"For, lo, the winter is past, the rain is over and gone. The flowers appear on the earth, the time of singing has come, and the voice of the turtledove is heard in our land. The**

fig tree puts forth her green figs, and the vines with the tender grapes give a good smell. Arise My love My fair one and come away."

This is one of the most beautiful and encouraging and uplifting passages in scripture. It can be analyzed word for word, but just allow it to minister to you with all of its depth of joy and hope. Just take it as a whole and allow it to wash over you. It says, "look, things are surely going from winter to spring. The time of singing is coming."

Here is a description written by someone of Israel in the spring. "Everywhere the earth was beautifully green and carpeted with flowers. The air was fresh and balmy and laden with the sweet scents of spring. The sky was so blue, the mountains and plains looked so beautiful, the birds, insects, the wild flowers, the fresh balmy breeze, the sweet smells, the gentle sun, the black tents all combined to make one glad to be alive. Come here in the spring O traveler and not in the arid, dusty, burnt-up autumn."

Who has stood in the midst of a lovely garden and not felt their heart melting as that beauty brings a dim reflection of the beauty of the Lord.

Twas when the spousal time of May
Hangs all the hedge with bridal wreaths,
And air's so sweet the bosom gay
Gives thanks for every breath it breaths;
When like to like is gladly moved,
And each thing joins in spring's refrain,
Let those love now who never loved;
Let those who have loved love again.

Let's take a stroll through the garden as we listen and sing a most precious song written in 1913 by C. Austin Miles.

IN THE GARDEN
I come to the garden alone while the dew is still on the roses,
and the voice I hear falling on my ear, the Son of God discloses.

Refrain:
And He walks with me, and He talks with me, and He tells me I am His own,
And the joy we share as we tarry there, none other has ever known.

He speaks, and the sound of His voice is so sweet the birds hush their singing,
And the melody that He gave to me within my heart is ringing.

I'd stay in the garden with Him though the night around me be falling,
But He bids me go through the voice of woe; His voice to me is calling.

Verse 14 repeated – **"O my dove in the clefts of the rock, in the secret places of the cliff, let Me see your countenance, let Me hear your voice; for your voice is sweet and your countenance is lovely."**

"Cleft of the rock" = place of concealment. The bridegroom is begging his bride to lay aside her timidity, skittishness, embarrassment, self-doubt, undervaluing of self, fear, and shame. The Lord loves the sight of His people. The Bridegroom loves to look upon His bride. He longs for and loves her voice. He delights in our songs and in our prayers.

Revelation 5:8 – **"Now when He had taken the scroll, the four living creatures and the 24 elders fell down before the Lamb, each having a harp, and golden bowls full of incense, which are the prayers of the saints."** But Jesus is calling us beyond prayers, supplications and requests to a place of daily intimacy where we converse with Him as one who is there with us.

This entire Song of Solomon speaks to this. Jesus says over and over again, **"Behold you are fair my love, behold you are fair, you have doves eyes."** The bride voices over and over, **"Behold you are handsome my Beloved, yes pleasant."**

Verse 15 –**"Catch us the foxes, the little foxes that spoil the vineyards of our love, for our vines have tender grapes"**

There are some different interpretations given to this, but I lean to the following, especially in light of our goal of reflecting the intimate passion between the bride and Bridegroom.

The vineyards, beautiful with fragrant blossoms, point to the covenant of love, and the foxes and little foxes, which can destroy those vineyards, point to the great and little enemies, and adverse circumstances, which threaten to gnaw and destroy love in the blossom before it can reach the ripeness of full enjoyment. The idea of clearing the vineyards of predators well suits the general import of Song of Solomon.

Let the blossoming love of the soul be without injury and restraint. Let the rising faith and affection be carefully guarded. It is like a beautiful rose bud opening to reveal its glory, and then the beetles come and eat away at its beauty. So as the bride we cannot be slack in guarding our relationship with the Bridegroom.

Verse 16 –**"My Beloved is mine and I am His. He feeds His flock among the lilies."**

As we adopt this for ourselves we mean that as soon as we realized His tender, strong affection for us we felt we must have His friendship. His love is an everlasting force, ever active, beneficent in 10,000 ways. His love is irresistible. I do not possess Him simply with my hands. It is not something outside me. It is a possession within me. It has become part and parcel of my being. I possess Him as the branch possesses the root.

We are the bride of Christ and as such are co- possessor by marriage of all that belongs to the Bridegroom, and He is co-possessor of all that we have. His righteousness is mine; all of the Excellencies of Christ are mine. He has chosen to share with me all that He has (Remember – He chose me because he wanted to). His friends are my friends.

He is mine in absence, mine in presence, mine through life, mine in death, mine in the judgment, and mine at the marriage supper of the Lamb. I am secure and honored and happy, because my Beloved is mine.

He is my wisdom, my righteousness, my sanctification, and my redemption.

> The opening heavens around me shine
> With beams of heavenly bliss,
> While Jesus says that He is mine,
> And whispers I am His.

Jesus' love is not just a sentimental affection, although it is that, but His love for us is a desperate and practical love. Perhaps we can make an attempt to paraphrase His attitude as follows:

"I love them so much, I long for their relationship so strongly, I am so completely desperate for them, that I will endure their ugliness, their wretchedness, even their hatred, and will give My very life for them that they can become whole, that My suffering can result in their joy."

Verse 16b-**"He feeds His flock among the lilies."**

He is our Lord and He is our good Shepherd. He knows His own and His own know him. Once He gave His life for the sheep. Now He feeds them, and leads them on their way until they come to the lilies of paradise, the garden of the Lord.

He made each of us for Himself, to be His, to be the object of His passionate affection.

Verse 17 – **"Until the day is cool, and the shadows flee away, turn my Beloved, and be thou like a roe or a young hart upon the mountains of Bether."** Bether = separation.

This could mean in light of verse 1:5 and 2:15 that she is being responsible for her duties in the vineyard which will occupy her time until the evening, and brings a time apart from her lover. She invites Him to return like a gazelle, as He did before, skipping upon the mountains. Like the bride who finds it necessary to be separated from her lover for a time and longs for his rapid return.

In effect she is saying, "Go my friend and do what you do. I am unable to come, but I will delight in Your power and majesty." We might also see in this verse that she is in a crisis of faith and must face her failure to experience the life she longs to live. Restoration will come later, but for now she experiences a time of defeat.

In Matthew 14:26-33 is a stunning fulfillment of the allegory of Song of Solomon.
In this experience the disciples were in a boat traveling across the Sea of Galilee. Jesus was not with them. Half way across the sea, in the middle of the night, a sudden storm tossed them about with great fury. Then Jesus came down from the mountain walking on the water toward them. The disciples were very frightened, and

cried out, **"It is a ghost."** But Jesus calmed them with the words, **"Be of good cheer. It is I. Do not be afraid."** Peter answered him and said, **"Lord if it is You, command me to come to You on the water."** Jesus replied, **"Come."** So Peter climbed out of the boat and began walking on the water toward Jesus. But when he saw that the storm was fierce, he was afraid, and beginning to sink he cried out, **"Lord save me."** Immediately Jesus stretched out His hand and caught him, and said to him, **"O you of little faith, why did you doubt?"** This really happened. Jesus really was there, skipping upon the hills (waves). Jesus called to Peter, **"Come."** We know Peter was a bold one, but I imagine there must have been a scream in his heart, "Oh no, Jesus is calling my bluff!" But for a moment he overcame his fear, stepped out of the safety of the boat, and joined Jesus. This was a terribly frightening thing to do and Peter lost his focus. But Jesus was there to rescue him. What is the point? When the King invites us to come, we can presume upon His power to save. Even though Peter didn't make it all the way, I believe that Jesus was thrilled at the willingness of Peter to dare to trust Him, and His little faith statement was not a critical rebuke. Jesus was saying, **"O Peter, if you only knew what is possible. Trust Me and I will take you through places and events you never dreamed of, for with Me all things are possible."**

PRAYER

O, Sovereign King, Majestic Lord of all things, I long for the courage of the leap of faith, the joy of the victorious dance upon the stormy waves, upon the mountains and hills of my fears. Call me again, Lord. Don't give up on me. Sooner or later I will trust you.

CHAPTER 3

Verses 1-4 -This is presented in Song of Solomon as the bride's dream of separation, but we want to look at it not as a dream, but as a dream representing the reality of our individual bridal relationship with the Bridegroom.

In the aftermath of the Shulamite's hesitancy to follow the King she experiences a kind of restlessness, the fear that she has lost the one her heart desires.

"By night on my bed I sought the one I love; I sought Him, but I did not find Him. I will rise now, I said, and go about the city; in the streets and in the squares I will seek the one I love. I sought Him, but I did not find Him. The watchmen who go about the city found me, to whom I said, "Have you seen the one I love?" Scarcely had I passed by them when I found the one I love. I held Him and would not let Him go until I had brought Him to the house of my mother and into the chamber of her who conceived me."

Verse 5-**"I charge you O daughters of Jerusalem by the gazelles or by the does of the field, do not awaken love until it pleases."**

See chapter 2:7 for an explanation of this mysterious charge.

As we face our own fears, there is often a sense of unrest rooted in the fear that God will measure us by how we see ourselves, and that we will be judged unworthy of His affections. These feelings are often the recurrent accusations of the enemy and of our own minds, passing judgment on ourselves based on the faulty assumption that God has done so also. Outside of ministry by the Holy Spirit it is almost impossible for us to understand that His assessment is based on totally different information from what we see. He is gazing upon a bride who is fully formed, whose life is hidden in the life of His Son, and who therefore can embrace with total confidence the character we already have been given.

When the Spirit of God is inviting us to dance upon the waves of our failures, fears and disappointments, we say no. It is too frightening to go there. We can't bear the thought of facing all that "stuff". And so we focus on the mountains of difficulties instead of upon the strength of the king, and we say, "You go ahead, I'll be along some other time." And so we lose His presence and can't find that sweet voice anywhere. But we begin to miss Him knowing that at days end only His presence is going to be enough. So we swallow our fear and go out to find Him once again.

She wanders through the city, past the watchmen, seeking Him until she finds the one she loves. She clings to Him not wanting to let Him go until He promises to come to her home. And she goes to her home to await His arrival.

The next thing she sees is a royal cavalcade approaching her house. And she realizes that the King has sent for her.

Verses 6-11- "**Who is this coming out of the wilderness like pillars of smoke, perfumed with myrrh and frankincense with all the merchants fragrant powders.**
Behold it is Solomon's couch with sixty valiant men around it of the valiant of Israel. They all hold swords, being expert in war. Every man has his sword on his thigh because of the fear in the night.
Of the wood of Lebanon, Solomon the King made himself a carriage. He made its pillars of silver, its support of gold, its seat of purple; its interior paved with love by the daughters of Jerusalem.

Go forth-O daughters of Zion and seek King Solomon with the crown with which His mother crowned Him on the day of His engagement. The day of the gladness of His heart."
Suddenly all the fears are gone, her unfaithfulness is a distant memory, and she is swept up in the overwhelming realization that she is at the center of His heart. She is His focus on, **"The day of the gladness of His heart."**

"The day of the gladness of His heart," is a picture of Jesus' triumphant return to claim His Bride at the end of the age. But it also pictures His triumph at Calvary. (Hebrews 12:2) **"Enduring the cross for the joy that was set before Him."** His gladness is rooted in the anticipation that at the end of the journey, even as the Shulamite awaited the King, we also as his precious ones will be waiting His arrival.

The anguish of that long, almost despairing search was not in vain. When she found Him, she held Him fast and brought Him to her own home, into its inmost chambers. When we find Jesus we passionately cling to Him with a strong embrace of faith.

Now it may be that Jesus will hide Himself from us for a while to strengthen our faith, and that His absence will reveal to us our desperate need of Him. We must bring Him into our home, into the very inmost chambers of our heart.

John 14:23 – Jesus declared, **"If anyone loves Me, he will keep My word, and My Father will love him, and we will come to him and make our home with him."**

Psalm 91 – **"He who [brings the Lord into his home, into his inmost chambers] will abide under the shadow of the almighty."** This is the shelter that a mother bird gives her brood. As verse 4 states, **"He will cover you with His feathers and under His wings you will find refuge."**

The crown of thorns and the regal crown are one and the same. It is with the crown of suffering that Jesus purchased the bride who will become the glorious diadem of Isaiah 62:3-5, "**You shall be a crown of glory in the hand of the Lord, and a royal diadem in the hand of your God. And as the Bridegroom rejoices over the bride, so shall your God rejoice over you**."

PRAYER

O Jesus, how do I begin to think about this? The stunning realization that the day of Your crushing is the day of Your delight is beyond my ability to comprehend. Teach my heart, O God. I want to know You and the fellowship of Your sufferings and the power of Your resurrection that I may finally know what You have in your heart concerning me.

The bride approaches in a carriage sent for her. Oh the glory, the overwhelming joy of this. Jesus sends His own carriage for us to carry us to our wedding. We don't have to find a way to the wedding. Jesus sends His own carriage with 60 valiant men escorting it. What love, what affection. We are each so special, so precious to our Bridegroom. This is my personal feeling. The wedding will not be a mass affair. No, each bride will have her own intimate wedding. And I don't believe that Jesus will escort her from the carriage, but there will be someone else, (use your own imagination here) to escort her to the wedding hall where Jesus will be anxiously waiting for her.

Verses 9-11 describe the details of the carriage in which the bride is borne to the royal city. It is the Bridegrooms personal carriage. This gives emphasis to the honor bestowed upon the bride. The king has sent His own carriage to convey His bride to the palace, the carriage in which He Himself was carried. It was the Kings, but now the brides, for the King has given it to her.

The carriage has been made according to Jesus own plans with artistic skill and magnificence. It was made of the fragrant and imperishable cedar wood brought from Lebanon, the country of the bride. Its decorations were of the richest gold and silver, and the costly Tyrian purple. It's interior was paved with love. A gift of the daughters of Jerusalem.

The King sent His own guard to escort the bride to her new home. King David had a guard of 30. Here is a guard of 60 mighty warriors, all-expert in war. The escort was given not just for honor, but also to assure the brides safe arrival to the wedding.

Psalm 91:11 – **"He will give His angels charge over you to keep you in all your ways."**

I Peter 1:3-5 – **"All honor to God, the God and Father of our Lord Jesus the Christ, for it is His boundless mercy that has given us the privilege of being born again so that we are now members of God's own family. Now we live in the sure hope of eternal life because Jesus rose from the dead." And God has reserved for His children the priceless gift of eternal life. It is kept in Heaven for you, pure and undefiled, beyond the reach of change and decay. And God in His mighty power will make sure that you get there safely to receive it because you are trusting Him. It will be yours in that coming last day for all to see. So be truly glad."**

THERE IS A GREAT AND GLORIOUS WEDDING RECEPTION COMING.

When Jesus, the true Solomon, the Prince of Peace shall bring His bride, the church, to the heavenly Jerusalem, He will manifest Himself to her in His glory. Now He is interceding for us that we may be with Him where He is, that we may behold His glory. Then we will see Him as He is, and shall be made like unto Him.

It was a great thing for the poor bride of Lebanon to be brought into the court of the king whose magnificence filled the Queen of Sheba with wonder and delight. But, **"Eye has not seen, nor ear heard, neither have entered into the heart of man, the things which God has prepared for them that love Him."** I Corinthians 2:9.

The heart of man cannot conceive the exceeding great joy of that moment of most entrancing bliss, when the heavenly Bridegroom will bring home His bride.

Verse 11 – **"Go forth O daughters of Zion, and see King Solomon with the crown with which his mother crowned him on the day of His engagement. The day of the gladness of His heart."**

As Isaiah said in Chapter 62:5, **"As the Bridegroom rejoices over the bride, so shall thy God rejoice over thee." You will no longer be called forsaken, neither shall your land anymore be called desolate, but you shall be called Hephzi-bah (My delight is in her) and your land, Beulah (married) for the Lord delights in thee."**

Certainly God has infinite patience, but I'll bet that Jesus is very anxious for His bride, really anxious for that wedding day.

Hebrews 12:2 – **"It was for the joy set before Him that Jesus endured the cross." The Lord brings home the lost sheep rejoicing. He says, "rejoice with Me for I have found My sheep that was lost."**

"Rejoice with Me. Yes, rejoice with Me."

AMAZING LOVE

Nothing can show the depth and desperate love with which He yearned for our salvation, for our relationship of love with Him than the agony of Gethsemane, the awful anguish of the cross.

Isaiah 53:11 – **"He shall see of the travail of His soul, and shall be satisfied."**
He came down from Heaven seeking His bride. Now she is with Him in his glory. Now He is satisfied, His precious bride is home.

Psalm 30:11 – **"You have turned my mourning into dancing; You have put off my sackcloth and clothed me with gladness."**

With the following song you invite your Bridegroom to dance with you.

DANCE WITH ME

Dance with me, O lover of my soul, to the song of all songs
Romance me, O lover of my soul, to the song of all songs

Behold, You have come over the hills, upon the mountains
To me You have run, my Beloved; You've captured my heart

With you I will go for you are my love; you are My fair one
The Winter is past and the Springtime has come

CHAPTER 4

Verses 1-15 - As we look at this passage we begin to experience a feel for the kind of love that rages in Jesus for His bride. But this is only a dim reflection of His passion. When we begin to comprehend this it causes breathlessness. This is not just a nice poem, a story; it is your story and my story. This is the heart of Jesus concerning you and me.

To make this Song of Solomon a part of us, to come into an intimacy with Jesus, to see Him as our lovely Bridegroom, we must look at it as not from the heart of Solomon but from the heart of Jesus Himself. See it as a love song or love letter, but even better as wooing directly from Jesus to you personally. This is given to us in a language of strong feeling. It is good to sit at His feet and soak in His passionate affection for us.

The brides' beauty, purity, sweetness, and delightfulness are set forth in these verses with all the richness of oriental imagery. These verses lead us into a sunny garden of the half-tropical En-Gedi, to the breezy heights of Lebanon with the flowing streams that convert the desert into a paradise. Orchards of pomegranates, gardens overflowing with spicy fragrance, murmuring fountains. These all suggest the charms of the bride whom the King claims as His own.

Verse 7 – **"You are all fair my love and there is no spot in you."**

How can this be? How can I think these thoughts concerning myself? Ephesians 5:27 informs us that Jesus has in mind to, **"Present us to Himself as a glorious church, not having spot or wrinkle, or any such thing, but that it will be holy and without blemish."**

So in the heart and mind of God we who have received His love are already in this completed state. Jesus can speak these wonderful things over us without exaggeration because they are fact.

This declaration of our standing with God, of who we are in Christ Jesus, is the heart of the good news called the Gospel. It is so astounding that we have difficulty accepting it. The life-changing power of this truth in Song of Solomon and in the New Testament is centered in the fact that Jesus sees us and relates to us now in the light of His finished work through the cross, His death and resurrection.

His right hand and strong arm have won the victory. The goal is the perfection of His people as His bride. These words in Song of Solomon are not blind love or flattery, they are real and are confirmed with a price, the crucifixion.

Verse 6- **"Until the day breaks and the shadows flee away I will go My way to the mountain of myrrh and to the hill of frankincense"** This is reference to the suffering of Jesus and is presented in the very midst of his declarations of love. This is the sober truthful assessment of the ravished-heart of God who is fully prepared to do whatever is necessary to bring about His desired result. He embraced the sacrificial dimension of this plan before the foundation of the world. He saw you then as His bride.

Isaiah 62:5 declares **"And as the Bridegroom rejoices over the bride, so shall your God rejoice over you."** This is why He could relate to the disciples the way He did. A ragtag group of fishermen, tax collectors, and thieves – He could call them apostles. He saw people as they are in the beauty of holiness, not in the grip of the fallen world's evil. John, a son of thunder (son of tumult), understood. He was able to speak of himself as **"The disciple Jesus loves."** Why could he say that? Because he knew it was true. In the secret place of prayer, as we minister to Him we see the beauty of His person, that compels us to believe Him, and agree with His passion for us. Have we not always longed to believe that? Haven't we always, deep inside, longed to be loved like that? The stunning truth is – I am loved this way.

Verse 1 – **"Behold you are fair my love, behold you are fair. You have dove's eyes behind your veil. Your hair is like a flock of goats going down from Mount Gilead."** As we observed in chapter 1:15, the Bridegroom is declaring to her that in His view she, although still immature, has already reached the single-minded fervency of love that her heart desires. A dove has tunnel vision. This could be paraphrased as, "You have tunnel vision for Me only, and are not distracted with other affections and desires."

Again, we must look at the word "fair" by the spirit. There really are no words to bring out the depth of God's love for us. There just aren't any. The words we use are just a door through which we enter into the realm where we can begin to feel it.

Paul's prayer in Ephesians 3:17, **"I pray that Christ will be more and more at home in your heart, living within you as you trust in Him. May your roots go down deep into the soil of God's marvelous love, and may you be able to feel and understand as all of God's children should, how long, how wide, how deep, and how high His love really is and to experience this love for yourself."**

Now the Lord through Solomon does an excellent job of opening that door for us through the use of many word pictures to describe "fair". The Bridegroom rejoices over the bride. She is wholly His. He enumerates her beauties. (In the Eastern form of erotic, poetic language). Her beauties are very precious to Him. His great love leads Him to dwell on every characteristic.

Psalm 45:13 – **"The royal daughter is all glorious within the palace. Her clothing is woven with gold. She shall be brought to the King in robes of many colors. The virgins, her companions who follow her, shall be brought to You. With gladness and rejoicing they shall be brought. They shall enter the Kings palace."**

Verse 2, 3 – **"Your teeth are like a flock of shorn sheep which have come up from washing, every one of which bears twins, and none is barren among them. Your lips are like a strand of scarlet, and your mouth is lovely. Your temples behind your veil are like a piece of pomegranate."**

<u>Don't lose sight of the fact here that this is personal. You are the bride. This is the Lord's picture of you.</u>

We could look at each one of the bride's beauties and try to describe what each characteristic means, but I believe this would just distract us from a true, deep spiritual understanding. I don't believe there is anyone who we could describe whose teeth are like a flock of shorn sheep, and whose temples are like a piece of pomegranate in a physical sense. But we could certainly use these types of words and understand in our hearts what feeling they were intended to convey. The poets are very good at it. And the most excellent poet, Jesus, knows exactly what He is saying.

Men, please don't feel embarrassed by the language used in this love song in the female gender, or by its reference to the "bride". All believers, male and female, are in actual fact, the bride of Christ.

Granted, men may have difficulty relating to being the bride, and to the erotic, female language. But it is all-spiritual. Men, you are fair, you do ravish the Lord's heart. Allow it to happen. Think of yourself as the beautiful bride. It is the truth.

Verse 4 – **"Your neck is like the tower of David built for an armory on which hang a thousand bucklers, all shields of mighty men."**

A strange way to describe the bride's beauty. But here is a change in the nature of the Bridegrooms' praise, because the bride is perfect in all her countenance. He does not forget to praise the majesty of His bride. This description suits a royal queen. She is full of dignity and grace in her bearing.

Verse 5 – **"Your two breasts are like two fawns, twins of a gazelle, which feed among the lilies."**

This is a delicate figure describing lovely equality and perfect contour and freshness of the bride's bosom. The meadow covered with lilies suggests beauty and fragrance. Put it this way. A twin pair of young gazelles lying in a bed of lilies suggests a fragrant delicacy and elegance.

Verse 6 – **"Until the day breaks and the shadows flee away, I will go my way to the mountain of myrrh, and to the hill of Frankincense."** Chapter 2:17 provides some details on this.

Verse 7 – **"You are all fair my love and there is no spot in you."** This verse 7 was described at the beginning of this Chapter 4.

Verse 8 – **"Come with Me from Lebanon My spouse. Look from the top of Amana, from the top of Senir and Hermon, from the lions dens, from the mountains of the leopards."**

The most likely meaning seems to be simply the Bridegroom rejoicing over the bride, and it means. "Give yourself up to Me – you are Mine. Look away from the past and delight yourself in the future." It could mean in the spiritual sense, the life we live without Christ is at best a life among the wild, untamed impulses of nature, and in the rough and dangerous places of the world. Jesus invites us to go with Him to the place that He has prepared for us. This is a difficult passage to pin down, but if we see it as above, it fits within our desire to come into intimacy with our Savior, Lord and Bridegroom.

Verses 9-15 – Before looking at verses 9-15 in detail just read and meditate on them, let them soak in and allow these affectionate words to enter your very inmost being. This beautiful passage stands by itself. And of course it is Jesus the Bridegroom speaking.

Verses 9-11 **"You have ravished My heart My sister, My spouse, you have ravished My heart with one look of your eyes, with one link of your necklace. How fair is your love, My sister My spouse? How much better than wine is your love, and the fragrance of your perfumes than all spices. Your lips O My spouse drip as the honeycomb. Honey and milk are under your tongue, and the fragrance of your garments is like the fragrance of Lebanon."**

Now we can glean some more of Jesus love for us out of these words that more and more of that love may just build up within us and fill us with a passion for our Bridegroom.

As we look at the fishermen of Galilee, the 12 disciples, that rough, self-centered bunch, we can see a love in bloom. The scripture says, not withstanding their glaring misconduct, **"Jesus loved them to the end."** And as love bloomed within them, we see John resting his head upon the breast of Jesus, and all except Judas giving their lives for him. John 13:23 – **"Now there was reclining on Jesus' breast one of His disciples whom Jesus loved."**

Sometimes when we can enter into a deep, intimate presence with the Lord and get a sense of how highly He regards our poor love for Him, it staggers our mind, seals our lips and takes our breath away. But nevertheless it is a fact. As full of blemish and imperfection as we are, He still counts us as jewels, His choicest possessions. With His generous heart He sets high value on our love for Him and in this way encourages us to give Him more.

We know that our Lord has many sources of joy in Heaven, but His enjoyment of His precious bride is the choicest. The love of His ransomed ones is His rare, sweetest joy. Once we were lost to Him, but now He has found us.

Can we even have the smallest sense of how our love returned to Him melts His heart? Maybe we can start to feel it when we recall what happened to our emotions, to our hearts when one of our precious little ones jumps up on our lap, throws their arms around our neck and sweetly says, "Daddy or Mommy, I love you."

Verse 11 – The Bridegroom speaks to His precious one, **"Your lips, O my spouse, drip as the honeycomb, honey and milk are under your tongue."**

The richest and sweetest of all honey is that which drips freely and first from the honeycomb. Like so the words of our fresh, warm love, are very sweet in the ear of Jesus.

As stated at the beginning, the purpose for walking through the Song of Solomon is one not necessarily of learning, but of impartation. To provide a foundation for the Lord to bring us into that sweet fellowship, that secret place, that intimacy with our Bridegroom. An intimacy that is expressed He to us and we to Him. Two lovers.

Verse 11 continued – **"The fragrance of your garments is like the fragrance of Lebanon."** The scent of pine trees and cedar forests is very pleasant, and Lebanon surpassed all other forests in Palestine. The word garments as used here in the Bible is referring to human activities, the things we do wherever we go. One of the lessons here is that Jesus finds pleasure in all that we do, however trivial and insignificant.

It is fitting to repeat here the beautiful story of mutual love found in Luke 7: 36-48.
"Then one of the Pharisees asked Jesus to eat with him. And Jesus went to the Pharisee's house and sat down to eat. And behold a woman in the city who was a sinner, when she knew that Jesus sat at the table in the Pharisee's house, brought an alabaster flask of fragrant oil and stood at Jesus' feet behind Him weeping. And she began to wash His feet with her tears and wiped them with the hair of her head. And she kissed His feet and anointed them with the fragrant oil. Now when the Pharisee saw this he thought to himself, saying, "This man, if He were a prophet, would know who and what manner of woman this is who is touching Him, for she is a sinner."

And Jesus, knowing his thought, said to him, **"Simon, I have something to say to you. There was a certain creditor who had two debtors. One owed $80,000 and the other $8,000. And when they had nothing with which to repay, he freely forgave them both. Tell me, therefore, which of them will love him more?" Simon answered, "I suppose the one whom he forgave more." Jesus answered, "You have rightly spoken."**

Then Jesus turned to the woman and said to Simon, **"Do you see this woman, I entered your house and you gave Me no water for My feet, but she has washed My feet with her tears and wiped them with the hair of her head. You gave Me no kiss but this woman has not ceased to kiss My feet since the time I**

came in. You did not anoint My head with oil, but this woman has anointed My feet with fragrant oil. Therefore I say to you, her sins, which are many, are forgiven, for she loved much. But to whom little is forgiven, the same loves little." And He said to her, "Your sins are forgiven."

I know a dear lady, a missionary now, whom years ago was a drug-addicted prostitute, kind of like in this Bible incident. One day she was literally lying, passed out, in a filthy gutter. Jesus reached down, lifted her, saved her, and cleansed her inside and outside. Now when He speaks to her He affectionately calls her "little one".

Verse 12 – **"A garden enclosed is My sister, My spouse, a spring shut up, a fountain sealed."**

The church, the Bride of Christ, is likened to a garden. It is a territory, enclosed, separated from the rest, separated from evil, and separated as a means of blessing. When we stroll through a garden our eyes delight in the many varieties of lovely flowers, bold colors, bright reds and yellows, delicate blooms, delicate in color and delicate in texture and design. And the sweet fragrance as it drifts by stirs up love within our hearts. As in a lovely garden we find great delight and solace, so in this sacred garden Jesus has a special joy. He calls it, My garden, My people, My sister, My spouse, a language of endearment.

Now here is a connection. Every plant, every tree, every blossom has been planted by Jesus himself. The unfolding of every blossom He is watching with delight. And He waters and prunes and cares for each one. He has a green thumb. He is a master gardener. And as the buds turn into beautiful blossoms, His delight becomes ecstasy. The blossoms are His bride, you and I.

This is a garden enclosed. It is inaccessible to thieves and wild beasts. This enclosed garden can be likened to a sheepfold. In the

East the sheep follow the shepherd into the sheepfold for the night. Then the shepherd lies at the entrance so the sheep can't leave and the wolves can't enter.

What does the Bible say? The new life of the child of God, of the bride is, **"Hid with Christ in God."** As a spring or a fountain has its source far down in the secret caverns of the earth, so we have our roots deep within Christ. As Paul prayed in Ephesians 3:16, **"May your roots go down deep into the soil of God's marvelous love."**

Verse 13 –15 – As our lives are hidden with Jesus, as we come into that intimate place with Him, all of these attributes become ours. Our Bridegroom not only enjoys them in us, but they flow out from us. We are a reflection of our Bridegroom, and it is like Jesus with great joy saying, **"This is my bride, see how lovely she is. She is an orchard of pomegranates and many pleasant fruits; she has the fragrance of henna with spikenard, and saffron, and calamus and cinnamon. And with her are not only the sweet perfume, but also the healing of frankincense, myrrh and aloes with all the spices. She is a well of living waters, streams from Lebanon."**

Every one of these attributes, every wholesome fruit within us He Himself has planted. Jesus said, **"I am glorified in them."**

Verse 16 –Chapter 5:1 – **"Awake, O north wind, and come, O south, blow upon my garden that its spices may flow out. Let my beloved come to His garden and eat its pleasant fruits." "I have come to My garden, My sister, My spouse. I have gathered My myrrh with My spice. I have eaten My honeycomb with My honey. I have drunk My wine with My milk."**
"Eat, O friends. Drink, yes drink deeply, O beloved ones."

All through Chapter 4 the bridegroom praises his brides beauty, and in Verse 12 describes her as a garden enclosed. In verse 16 she invites the Bridegroom to come into the garden. She says, **"Let my beloved come to His garden."** It is His garden that He gave to her. In effect she is saying, "Come to Your garden and eat of the pleasant fruits which You have planted and tended. This is the fruit You have produced in me. Come now and let us savor it together." Every blossom has been under His loving care. She offers them back to her Bridegroom..

You too can invite Jesus to come to His garden and meet you there. And you can experience the beautiful words of the song, In The Garden. "He walks with me and He talks with me and He tells me I am His own. And the joy we share as we tarry there none other has ever known."

Now it appears that some others have wandered by the garden. Perhaps they are the Daughters of Jerusalem, the friends of the bride. But whoever they are He invites them in and encourages them, **"Eat, O friends. Drink, yes drink deeply O beloved ones."** He addresses them as, beloved and as friends. Jesus uses tender names to address His friends.

In Chapter 4, the Bridegroom refers to His bride as, **"my sister, my spouse."** Again in 5:2 this is repeated. This is a term not only of endearment but also of commitment. Why is the word sister used? In some ancient cultures it was the practice for the husband to adopt his wife as his sister, thus forming a stronger marriage bond. Here in this context it is even stronger. In marriage (my spouse) the bride and Bridegroom become one flesh. When adopted as a sister, the bride becomes one with the family also. For us in our marriage to Jesus we become one spirit with Him, and we also become a member of God's greater family.

CHAPTER 5

Verse 1 – Here the Bridegroom replies to His bride's invitation, **"I have come to My garden, My sister, My spouse."**

In Revelation 3:20 the Bridegroom pleads, **"Behold, I stand at the door and knock, whoever hears My voice and opens the door, I will come in and dine with them and they with Me."**

The bride's invitation is received and the Bridegroom comes, and they enjoy each other within the surroundings of the beautiful garden.

In Isaiah 65:24 the Lord makes a promise to all who call upon Him, **"Before they call I will answer, and while they are still speaking I will hear."**

Verses 2-8 – **"I sleep but my heart is awake, it is the voice of my Beloved. He knocks saying, "Open for Me, My sister, My love, My dove, My perfect one, for My head is covered with dew, My locks with the drops of the night."** The bride continues her response.

"I have taken off my robe. How can I put it on again? I have washed my feet. How can I defile them? My Beloved put His hand by the latch of the door, and my heart yearned for Him. I arose to open for my Beloved, and my hands dripped with myrrh, my fingers with liquid myrrh on the handles of the lock. I opened for my Beloved, but He had turned away and was gone. My heart went out to Him when He spoke. I sought Him but I could not find Him. I called to Him but He gave me no answer. The watchmen who went about the city found me. They struck me, they wounded me. The keepers of the walls

took my veil away from me. I charge you, O Daughters of Jerusalem, if you find my Beloved, that you tell Him I am lovesick."

As in Chapter 3, this is also presented as the bride's dream of separation, but as we did in Chapter 3, let's look at it not as just a dream but as a dream representing the reality of our individual relationship with the Bridegroom. These verses give us a forward looking prophecy, a video if you will of the spiritual cycle of each of our lives, of the ups and downs in our love relationship with our Bridegroom, our Husband. We see a movie of our slip into apathy, our carelessness, and the unwavering patience, pursuit, unyielding passion of our Lover.

"I sleep but my heart is awake."

The Bridegroom is absent, the bride is alone. The bride is sleeping when she should be awake and watching for the Bridegroom. But her heart is awake. At the worst times of indifference there is always some dim consciousness of His presence, always some faint love for Him. He said He would never leave us nor forsake us. This is why we rejoice in Him. He is so beautiful, so wonderful because no matter how estranged from Him, no matter how backslidden, He will never cast us aside, never give up on us. Even though we lose our faith He remains faithful because He cannot deny Himself as it states in II Timothy 2:13.

These statements in II Timothy 2 are a stumbling block for many. **"If we died with Him, we shall also live with Him. If we endure we shall also reign with Him. If we deny Him He will also deny us. If we are faithless, He remains faithful for He cannot deny Himself."**

We rejoice over His faithfulness, but then the accuser reminds us of that statement, **"If we deny Him He will deny us,"** and our joy turns to fear because we know our weakness, and are afraid that someday under trying circumstances it is quite possible that we will deny Him, and then He will deny us, or maybe we are reminded of times when we have already denied Him. And now our bridegroom's invitation, **"Eat O friends and drink, drink deeply, O lovers,"** loses its sweetness. And we will retreat back to the deadly attitude that His passion for me is dependent upon me, upon my being good enough and strong enough. And this is devastating.

We can allow that as we deny Him we will lose intimate fellowship with Him, our precious relationship will suffer. But as the closing statement of that triplet confirms, "He remains faithful." And even within us the fire may be out but the coals continue to glow.

We cannot deny ourselves. The spark is always there, and the author of our faith has promised to finish that which He started.

Jude 1:1 – **"To those who are called, sanctified by God the Father, and preserved in Christ Jesus."** Or we can say, kept in the faith by Christ Jesus.

Peter is proof of the Lord's passionate faithfulness. Peter made an impassioned commitment to Jesus to even die with Him if necessary, that he would never disown Him. We all know that Peter denied Jesus three times in the strongest sense, even with an oath. "Are you people deaf, what is wrong with your hearing, I told you, and I tell you again, I do not, do not, do not know Him." John Chapter 18.

But Jesus remained faithful to Peter for relationship with Jesus does not depend on our own fallible character, but on His flawless and faithful nature. Jesus not only restored this terribly fallen and broken, unfaithful man to fellowship, but gave him a place of leadership in the church.

Romans 5:8-11 – "**But God demonstrated His love toward us in that while we were still sinners Christ died for us. For if when we were enemies we were reconciled to God through the death of His son, much more having been reconciled, we shall be saved by His life.**"

In John 14:1,2 Jesus said, "**In My Fathers house are many mansions. If it were not so I would have told you. I go to prepare a place for you.**"

In I Peter 1:4-6 God's faithfulness is again guaranteed. "**And God is protecting for His children the priceless gift of eternal life, it is kept in heaven for you, pure and undefiled, beyond the reach of change and decay. And God in His mighty power will make sure that you get there safely to receive it, because you are trusting Him. It will be yours in that coming last day for all to see. So be truly glad.**"

In John 14:1,2 ,Jesus gave this promise, "**Let not your heart be troubled, you believe in God believe also in Me. In My Father's house are many mansions. If it were not so I would have told you. I go to prepare a place for you. And if I go to prepare a place for you, I will come again and receive you to Myself that where I am you will be also.**"

Well, we went through all of this because if we are not convinced that we are preserved in Christ, it will destroy our ability to drink deeply.

But let's return to the Shulamite for there is much more the Lord, the Bridegroom, wants to reveal to us of His fiery passion for His bride. We have looked at just one line of verse 2.

The bride confessed that she was sleeping, but she had one eye open so to speak. Her heart was awake. Because she had set her love upon Him she could hear His call of love even while in a state of slumber.

"It is the voice of my Beloved, my heart wakens to listen."

Through the eyes of the Shulamite we see ourselves. We can relate to her in her weakness, in her passionate love for the Bridegroom, which sometimes fluctuates, but never dies.

The Lord expected her to be awake when He came, and He knew she was sleeping, and was probably disappointed. But He comes full of tenderness.

"Open to Me, My sister, My love, My dove, My perfect one." He still calls his bride, My sister, as He did before the cloud had come upon her love. He still says, My love, My dove, as he said before. And He now has a fresh term of endearment, which He hasn't used before, **"My perfect one, My undefiled one."**

He knocks and asks her to open the door that He may enter.

To bring this home to us, look at Mark 14:32-38 where we see a terrible testimony to the weakness of man – to our individual weakness, and to the compassionate understanding of Jesus. This is when Jesus went into the garden to pray just before His betrayal, trial, and crucifixion.

"Then they (his disciples) came to a place named Gethsemane, and He said to his disciples, "sit here while I pray." Then He took Peter, James and John with Him, and He began to be troubled and deeply distressed. He said to them, "My soul is exceedingly sorrowful, even to death. Stay here and watch." He went a little farther and fell on the ground, and prayed that

if it were possible, the hour might pass from Him. And He said, "Abba Father, all things are possible for You. Take this cup away from Me, nevertheless not what I will, but what You will." Then He came and found them sleeping and said to Peter, "Simon are you sleeping. Could you not watch one hour. Watch and pray, lest you enter into temptation. The spirit is truly ready, but the flesh is weak." Again He went away and prayed and spoke the same words. And when He returned, He found them asleep again, for their eyes were heavy, and they did not know what to answer Him. Then He came the third time and said to them, "Are you still sleeping and resting. It is enough. The hour has come. Behold I am being betrayed into the hands of sinners. Rise up, let us go. See My betrayer is at hand."

What a dreadful thing they did, how ugly. They had been with the Savior for three years, ate with Him, sat at His feet, sweated with Him. Peter even boasted how he would never desert Jesus, even die with Him. John had lovingly laid his head on the breast of Jesus. And yet, in the hour of their friend's greatest need, the hour of His agony, they couldn't even keep their eyes open.

Jesus could have, justifiably, strongly rebuked them or shouted in exasperation, "You men just don't have it, you will never amount to anything." This of course would have destroyed them.

The Lord did chide them, but in that there was a word of encouragement. He said, **"Simon are you sleeping.? Could you not watch one hour? Watch and pray lest you enter into temptation for the spirit is truly ready, but the flesh is weak."** Even in the midst of his agony, Jesus was still concerned about their welfare.

And tragically the Lord's agony in the garden ends with betrayal by Judas, the flight of the disciples, and Peter's denial that He even knew Jesus. Don't we often look at our Redeemer's sufferings in a drowsy manner and instead of being ready to die with Him, we are not even prepared to watch with Him one hour. Now I share this with you certainly not to put a burden on you or condemn you. This is just the opposite of what Song of Solomon wants to impart to us.

Just before Jesus gave up His spirit He looked out in the crowd, saw His Mother and the disciple, John, and said **"Woman behold your son,"** and to John, **"Behold your Mother."** There was no thought of the drowsiness and betrayal by His disciples. He trusted John to take care of Mary.

And in despair the disciples went fishing, and in the morning they saw Jesus on the beach, but didn't know it was He. Listen to these tender words as Jesus called out to them. **"Children, have you any food?"** He called them "children", a word of great affection, tenderness, passion, and warmth.

He had appeared to the disciples prior to this time also, and Jesus never chided them. He never said, "Now listen guys, we need to talk about your poor behavior back there in the garden."

As we review these events in the garden and the courtyard during the trial, and at His resurrection, there are no guilt feelings placing a barrier between the disciples and Jesus. Peter had his bitter time of repentance and then returned to the Lord. Sometimes we refuse to receive the Lord's forgiveness, to forgive ourselves.

And one of the most poignant passages in the Bible is when in that boat they finally recognized that the one on the beach was Jesus. John cried out, **"It is the Lord."** We can visualize him jumping up and down in the boat like a gleeful child and shouting over and over, **"It is the Lord."** His soul was so filled with love and excitement that he couldn't contain it.

And of course, the unrestrained, exuberant Peter wasn't about to hang around in that boat until they could row to shore. As the scripture says, **"He plunged into the sea, and swam to shore."**

And when they all had arrived, Jesus said to them, **"Come and eat breakfast."** What wonderful fellowship, **"Come and eat breakfast." "Come children, come and share breakfast with Me."**

This passage is so precious because sometimes in frustration or disappointment we say "I'm going fishing." But then in time our "Friend" shows up and says, **"come and eat, I have food prepared for us."**

As we continue in Verses 2 and 3 the Bridegroom says, **"My head is covered with dew, my locks with the drops of the night." The bride replies, "But I have taken off my robe, how can I put it on again, I have washed my feet, how can I defile or dirty them."**

We need to expand the sense of Verses 2 and 3 in order to discover the full meaning. The Bridegroom asks His bride to open the door that He may enter. Of course Jesus is the Bridegroom and these verses are a representation of Jesus' passion. He has been wandering in the darkness, and as when He came unto his own there was no room for Him in the inn, and as during the days of His earthly ministry, He had not a place to lay his head. So now He knocks at one door after another and heart after heart is closed against Him. They will not open that He may enter and make His abode with them.

Now He comes to His sister bride asking her as if for His own sake portraying the unutterable depth of His infinite, self-abasing love, **"Open to Me, My sister, My love, My dove, My perfect one."**

He pleads as for Himself, as if He needed shelter, **"My head is filled with dew, and My locks with the drops of the night."**

DESPERATE LOVE.

The bride does not realize the deep, solemn meaning of the Bridegrooms' call. She is still half asleep. In her spiritual slumber she makes poor excuses and will not rise and open until it is too late. She will not take a little trouble for the sake of the one she loves. Her love for Him has not grown cold, she just doesn't want to make the effort right now to respond to His plea. Sound familiar?

"I have taken off my robe, how can I put it on again? I have washed my feet, how can I dirty them?"

But her Lover continues to appeal to her and seeks to open the door. **"My Beloved put His hand by the latch of the door."** He had just come from the garden where His hands had been dipped in myrrh. As He tried the latch some of this myrrh was left on the latch.

His plea finally awoke in her the fear that she would lose Him by her coldness and selfish neglect, and her heart yearned for Him. She arose to open the door for Him now, and as her hand closed around the latch, her hand dripped with the liquid myrrh left there by His hand. The love, the passion within Him for his bride was so intense that even His touch upon the wood and metal of the door left a liquid coating of the love. But as she opened the door expecting Him to still be there, He was gone. What a dreadful moment. "Oh, what have I done, where has He gone." Her soul must have failed her – she was helpless, she was lost. It must have been as if her very soul fled from her, leaving her limp, without hope or life. Have you ever been there?

The house is empty. To lose Him is to lose everything, to lose life itself.

But now she remembered how her soul went out to Him at the sound of His voice. Remember Verse 2, **"I sleep but my heart is awake, it is the voice of my Beloved."** This was not some stranger knocking on her door. This was the one she dearly loved, her Bridegroom. Then she aroused herself. It was time to act to stir up the passion within her for her lover. And she said, **"I sought Him, but I could not find Him. I called to Him but He gave me no answer."**

Just thinking about the loneliness the agonizing desperation she felt, makes my soul cry out within me. "I have lost the most precious part of my life, actually life itself." For there is no life without Him. The desperation is beyond words. If you ever felt this you know what I mean.

Sometimes our Bridegroom will withdraw Himself to make us realize that life is blank without Him to make us cry out like Job, **"Oh that I were as in months past, as in the days when God preserved me; when His candle shined upon my head, and when by His light I walked through darkness, as I was in the days of my youth, when the secret of God was upon my tabernacle."** Job29:1- 4.

"He hides himself," Job said, **"I cannot see Him."** But Job continues to trust in his Beloved even in the midst of darkness. He confessed, **"But He knows the way that I take. When He has tried me, I shall come forth as gold."**
No matter what the circumstances, we are His precious bride and our Bridegroom will never desert us. This is His unbreakable covenant with us.

At the cross, Jesus was rejected so that we can now be secure.

So she went out to search for Him. She said, **"The watchmen who went about the city found me. They struck me, they wounded me. The keepers of the walls took my veil from me."**

This is a difficult passage. What does it mean? How does it relate to our quest to walk in intimacy with Him?

Remember in Chapter 3 a similar incident? There the watchmen had not been unfriendly, even though they apparently were unable, or unwilling, to help her in her search.

We can understand these experiences for us personally, particularly the later unpleasant experience, from two points of view:

1. Difficulties will arise in our search after intimacy with Jesus – sometimes danger and persecution. **"We must through much tribulation enter into the Kingdom of God." Acts 19:22.**
2. Or we can look at it this way. We must be always watchful. Jesus bids not out of a harsh demand but as a compassionate warning to help us, knowing our weakness. **"Watch therefore, for you know not when the master of the house will come, in the evening, or at midnight, or at the cockcrowing, or in the morning, lest coming suddenly He finds you sleeping. And what I say to you I say to all. Watch."** Mark 13:35–37. Remember, the bride was sleeping.

We must heed the prayer of the child Samuel, "**Speak Lord, for your servant hears."** I Samuel 3:9.

The two incidents of sleep, in Chapter 3 and here in Chapter 5 instruct us that each time we refuse to listen, the old sleepiness steals more and more over our souls, our slumber becomes deeper, the difficulty of awakening becomes greater, repentance more doubtful, more surrounded with dangers, calling for more exertion of will, more determined effort.

This admonition from our Beloved Bridegroom in Mark 13 above is a pleading with us to be careful, not take His love for granted, because He knows we are but flesh subject to many temptations. He is protecting His precious bride. And so rather than demanding words they are words of loving concern of a jealous Bridegroom to His bride.

The bride could not find her Beloved. She seeks help from her friends. **"I charge you O daughters of Jerusalem, if you find my Beloved, that you tell Him I am lovesick."**

She had used the words, "**I am lovesick",** once before in Chapter 2:5. There the expression was used in the context of, **"His banner over me is love."** Then the joy of His love was almost too great for her, she was sick with His love. Now it is different. Now her longing for an absent Bridegroom produces a longing type of sickness, a heart sickness. She fondly thinks that if He only knew her yearning for Him He would return; He would forgive all that was in the past, and bring her again under the banner of His love. So we too, awakened out of sleep, long for the Savior's presence.

She feels that she is sick. Without Him all is dark. Without Him there is no spiritual health, no joy, no hope. She seeks Him in deep pleading, and calls for the intercession of friends, to bring her distress and longing before the throne. David once said, **"Besides Thee I desire nothing on earth."**

David knew this longing: Psalm 63 – **"O God you are my God; earnestly will I seek You. My soul thirsts for You, my flesh**

longs for You in a dry and thirsty land where there is no water."

Psalm 42 – **"As the deer pants for the water brooks, so pants my soul for You, O God. My soul thirsts for God, for the living God."**

What is our Beloved's response? What is his response always? **"Eat O friends and drink, drink deeply, my beloved."**

There is a beautiful song. AMAZING LOVE

I'm forgiven because You were forsaken
I'm accepted, You were condemned
I'm alive and well, Your spirit is within me
Because You died and rose again.

Amazing love, how can it be?
That You my King would die for me
Amazing love, I know it's true
And it's my joy to honor You
In all I do, I honor You

Verse 9 – The Daughters of Jerusalem now enter into the picture and sincerely quiz the bride. **"What is your Beloved more than another beloved oh fairest among women? What is your Beloved more than another beloved that you so charge us?"** To properly understand their questioning we need to include Verse 1 of Chapter 6. **"Where has your Beloved gone, oh fairest among women? Where has your Beloved turned aside that we may seek Him with you?"**

Remember in Chapter 1:4 we said that the Daughters of Jerusalem are caught up in the brides exultation of her lover and pronounce that they want to follow, that they want to share in the brides rejoicing, and that they too recognize the Bridegrooms' love as being better than wine.

The Living Bible states it this way: **"O woman of rare beauty, what is it about your loved one that is better than any other, that you command us (to tell Him you are lovesick)?"** The Shulamite then proceeds to describe her Beloved in all His attributes in Verse 10-17.

Verse 10 – **"White and ruddy, chief among 10,000."** Ruddy speaks of all the signs of health, vigor, maturity, and beauty. Nothing in Him is marred, there is no blemish, and He is utter perfection. Radiant, dazzling, brilliant, shining white. Brilliant in His loveliness, radiant in His splendor. The dazzling brilliance that surrounds the resurrected Christ's person is made up of all the bright colors, shining lights, exotic fragrances, awesome power, heavenly sounds and beautiful music.

He possesses indescribable beauty and splendor. He is unique and distinct in His beauty. Every color is set in perfect contrast to all the other colors. His city is dazzling like a perfect celestial diamond shining with brilliance as described in Revelation Chapter 4 verses 1-4.

In Song of Solomon 1:3 –**"Because of the fragrance of Your good ointments Your very name is ointment poured forth."** Jesus is drenched in lovely fragrances – not metaphors, but real. In II Corinthians 2:15a –"**For we are to God the fragrance of Christ."** Here we learn that the fragrance of Christ is also the fragrance of His bride.

In Verse 16, with adoring eyes of supernatural love, the bride beholds His perfection and cries, **"He's altogether lovely, and this is my Beloved."** White speaks of His divine nature. Ruddy speaks of His human nature. He has at the same time the fullness of deity and the fullness of humanity. God the Father and the angels are not like that. Jesus is completely unique.

Verse 11 – **"His head is like the finest gold."** This is symbolic, spiritual language. In this imagery is depicted the majesty and the divine excellence of Jesus. It suggests the highest degree of quality and excellence imaginable. The finest gold has no impurities, and Jesus in His sovereignty has no impurities at all. He is the finest of the finest gold – the most pure and most precious possible. His head, His leadership, is the finest gold and can never be improved upon.

"His locks are wavy and black as a raven". This message is that Jesus' consecration to God and to his people is eternally vigorous. He never grows old, tired and weary. His bride can be wonderfully secure because He is forever in His prime and at the highest peak of His love, passion, and dedication.

Verse 12 – **"His eyes are like doves by the rivers of waters, washed with milk, and fitly set."**

Jesus sees all things so His eyes suggest his omniscience. Even things hidden in darkness are clear to Him. He sees both good and bad. When we understand that He thoroughly knows our bad stuff, then His shed blood is more precious than ever. It doesn't cause you to draw away but makes you praise and thank Him more. He also sees the cry in our hearts to love and obey Him. His eyes see our private longing for righteousness.

"Like doves" denotes singleness of vision and purity. A dove can only see straight ahead. A dove also speaks of purity and the Holy Spirit.

The **"Rivers of waters"** are where the doves bathe and become clean. Jesus interprets what He sees through eyes unclouded by

any uncleanness. There is no distortion in the interpretation of the facts that He sees. His eyes express feeling and devotion.
"Washed with milk" speaks of His simplicity and innocence. He is at one time both the Lion and the Lamb. The childlike and the complex.

"His eyes are fitly set." With no deformity, like a jewel set perfectly by a most skillful artist when constructing a priceless piece of jewelry. His vision and knowledge are perfect, being neither farsighted nor nearsighted.

Verse 13 –**" His cheeks are like a bed of spices, like banks of scented herbs. His lips are lilies dripping liquid myrrh."**

The cheeks reveal the internal emotional state and reveal the inner beauty of the countenance. Jesus' cheeks are like a garden of beautiful, fragrant spices. A **"Bed of spices"** indicates the diversity of His passion, pleasures and delights.

Banks of scented herbs speaks of the extravagant fragrance and multitudes of His affections. Sweet smelling flowers in full blossom produce a most delightful garden. This is the emotional makeup of Jesus – His passion for us, His longing for us and His delight in us. It also speaks of Jesus' delight in His Father and the Father's delight in His Son, and of their passion and pleasure over their creation.
"His lips are lilies dripping liquid myrrh." Lilies are sweet and satisfying – Psalm 19:10, **"His words are sweeter than honey and the honeycomb."**

Myrrh is an herb used for incense, perfume, and medicine and embalming. It is antiseptic and has a bitter taste. It is one ingredient of the holy anointing oil. It has a sweet fragrance with a bitter taste. The primary reference here is to perfume. His word is perfume to my soul as above in Psalm 19. Also Psalm 45, which is a psalm to Jesus the great King, in Verse 8, **"All your garments are scented with myrrh, aloes, and cassia."**

There could also be a companion meaning of "tough love" as sometimes in the interest of correction, His word will be bitter to us. But even here the bitterness, chastening, rebuke, is given in love such that we may receive cleansing from the sin that is preventing us from smelling the sweet perfume.

Mark 9:2-6 – **"Jesus took Peter, James and John to the top of a mountain. No one else was there. Suddenly His face began to shine with glory, and His clothing became dazzling white, far more glorious than any earthly process could ever make it. Then Elijah and Moses appeared and began talking with Jesus. "Teacher, this is wonderful," Peter exclaimed. "We will make three shelters here, one for each of you." He said this just to be talking for he didn't know what else to say and they were all terribly frightened."**

At the transfiguration Jesus opens the eyes of His trusted friends, Peter, James and John, allowing them to see the truth of His identity, undisguised in servant garments. They see Him for who He really is and are stunned. One reason the disciples were invited to this glorious event was that they could be strengthened in the reality of a beauty they had yet to experience here on earth. The revelation of His beauty to us through Song of Solomon and to some by vision, is for our exhilaration. It serves as an anchor for our faith and helps us to understand the joy that awaits us as we long to see Jesus face to face.

Psalm 27:1 – **"One thing I have desired of the Lord, that will I seek, that I may dwell in the house of the Lord all the days of my life, to behold the beauty of the Lord."**

Verses 14, 15 – **"His hands are rods of gold set with beryl. His body is carved ivory inlaid with sapphires. His legs are pillars of marble set on bases of fine gold. His countenance is like Lebanon, excellent as the cedars."**

The comparison with works of ivory refers to the perfect smoothness and symmetry as of a beautiful ivory statue, the work of the highest artistic excellence. So in the description of the legs there is the combination of white and gold, the white marble setting forth greatness and purity, and the gold sublimity and nobleness. This suggests that in the royal Bridegroom there is personal beauty united with kingly majesty.

The description in all of these verses is of the body in outward appearance and figure, but the word itself signifies inward parts. The Bridegroom is total unbroken perfection both inward and outward.

To some minds the descriptions in these verses and indeed the whole of Song of Solomon may be repellent. But to those to whom this is not so, the warmth and glow of the Eastern language is by no means too realistic. They usher in feelings of delight in the Lord with expressions in rapturous music.

As stated in the Introduction, the expressions of Song of Solomon are chaste, pure, romantic, delicate, sensuous, and always mysterious. They can be understood only with the heart.
Verse 16 – **"His mouth is most sweet. Yes He is altogether lovely. This is my Beloved, and this is my Friend O Daughters of Jerusalem."**

In these words is a description of the Bridegroom through the eyes of a lovesick bride. Prior to these words (Verse 10 – 15) the bride had extolled the majesty and beauty of the Bridegroom. In this verse she goes deeper, **"He is altogether lovely." "This is my**

Beloved and Friend." From the intimacy of the secret chambers of her heart, out of the depths of love and magnificent devotion, this exalted, heavenly song springs forth.

If we jump back to Verses 2-8 and especially Verses 6-8 the Shulamite is devastated. She could not find her Beloved. **"I sought Him but I could not find Him. I charge you O Daughters of Jerusalem, if you find my Beloved, that you tell Him I am lovesick."** Then she goes on to describe His majesty and loveliness.

To understand the heart of the lovesick bride in these passages is to see God in a depth that few of us find. But it is possible, and that is what the goal is here. As we behold our Bridegroom through the Shulamite's eyes, we pray that God will open the eyes of our understanding and illuminate our hearts.

We must take some reflective and meditation time here to seek the depths of these most precious words, "He is altogether lovely." The whole purpose of this commentary is to make these words intimately personal.

ALTOGETHER LOVELY

We have just looked at the attributes of our Bridegroom, King, and Savior. A review of the Shulamite's description plus a few of our own follows:
White and ruddy
Distinguished above all
His head like the finest gold
His locks are wavy
Eyes like doves
Cheeks like a bed of spices
His lips are lilies dripping liquid myrrh
His hands are rods of gold set with beryl

His body is carved ivory inlaid with sapphires
His legs pillars of marble set on bases of fine gold
His countenance excellent as the cedars of Lebanon
His mouth is most sweet
The spotless lamb
No faults or flaws
The desire of ages
King of Kings
Gloriously radiant
Tender shepherd

A summary of these verses 10-16:

The bride enumerates the various points of excellence, which together make up the completeness of the Bridegroom's beauty. The Christian loves to meditate upon the various graces which make up the holy beauty of the Bridegroom's character – His lowliness, His gentleness, His long-suffering kindness, His holy wisdom, His absolute unworldliness, His unselfish devotion, His meekness, His forbearance, His patience, His endurance, His calm and lofty courage, the majestic bearing which forced even the Roman soldiers to exclaim, "Truly this Man was the Son of God."

The Lord Jesus Christ, the Bridegroom, is the Desire of all nations. His mouth is all sweetness, both His holy words and His gracious looks. The look at His countenance that Jesus gave His disciples was a thing to be remembered all of their lives, full of heavenly meaning, full of divine love. The very tones of that most sacred voice surely had, and have, an indescribable sweetness. Jesus said unto her, **"Mary."** That one word was enough. The author of the song, In the Garden, knew that sweetness when he wrote, "He speaks and the sound of his voice is so sweet the birds hush their singing."

Who can tell the entrancing sweetness of the most blessed words, which with all our hearts deepest yearning we long one day to hear, **"Come, blessed children of My Father."**

These last words of the bride must be our very own, **"This is my Beloved and this is my Friend."** If He is indeed ours, our Beloved, our Friend, our Savior, then we have everything.

This song will give us an opportunity to express our own passion for our beloved Bridegroom:

I LOVE YOU LORD

I love You Lord
And I lift my voice
To worship You, Oh my soul rejoice

Take joy my King in what You hear
Let it be a sweet, sweet sound in Your ear

PRAYER

Lord God Almighty, show me Your glory. Let me see You even though my eyes are still far too dim for my satisfaction. Touch them, Lord, and cause me to behold Your beauty that I might exult in You and be settled in the truth. You are worthy of all praise, Jesus. Cause all nations to see your glory that the Lamb may receive the reward due His name.

CHAPTER 6

In Chapter 5 the bride exulted her lover, the **"chief among 10,000."** In this chapter the Bridegroom praises the beauty of His bride, **"lovely as Jerusalem."**

And here we find the Daughters of Jerusalem again. Remember in Chapter 5 the bride solicited their help in finding her Beloved, and they quizzed her with, "What is your Beloved more than another?" She then rolled out all His glorious attributes.

Now the Bridegroom has gone for a while. And in their question to her I believe it is not really a direct question but sort of a playful way to help her pour out her feelings.

Verse 1 – **"Where has your Beloved gone, O fairest among women. Where has your Beloved turned aside, that we may seek Him with you."**

Both the bride and the Daughters know where He is as evidenced in the next verse. **"My Beloved has gone to His garden to the beds of spices, to feed His flock in the gardens, and to gather lilies."** The bride is not as anxious as she was before when she begged the Daughters, **"Please help me find my Beloved because I am lovesick."**

There is no distress now in the language of the bride. She is not complaining and crying out in agony under a sense of desertion. She is confident of where He is and calmly sings of His perfect love even though He is absent from her. She knows He is where His perfect beauty and fragrance are.

Here is kind of an aside to the Daughters of Jerusalem's inquiry. The interlude couched in a little different language of another searcher; perhaps it is a tale of our own experience, or someone we know.

The searcher asked, "What is there in Jesus that makes Him so attractive?" To this question the disciple responded, answering the question fully, giving a full description of the sinner's Friend. He testified to the worth and excellence of the heavenly King. And now the inquirer asks further, "Where may I find this gracious Friend? My heart craves the good, which this Friend alone can bestow. I would have Him too. Tell me where I may find Him?"

In Verses 2 and 3 the bride states, **"My Beloved has gone to His garden to the beds of spices, to feed His flock in the gardens, and to gather lilies. I am my Beloved's, and my Beloved is mine. He feeds His flock among the lilies."**

"I am my Beloved's, and my Beloved is mine." This is a repeat of Chapter 2:16 after her brothers had talked about catching the little foxes that spoil the vine.

Now take a closer look at this further reference to the garden. There are several references to gardens in this beautiful book. The bride declared, **"My Beloved is gone down into His garden."**

On the part of a believer, a bride of Christ, there is no doubt where their Beloved can be found. It is in the garden that we meet our Beloved. In Chapter 5:1, He said, **"I have come to My garden, My sister My spouse."** Just before that in Chapter 4:12, He says, **"A garden enclosed is My sister My spouse ---."** The garden is the brides and the Bridegrooms together. It is our meeting place also where you and I can enjoy our Beloved Jesus. As the Word says, **"He is our inheritance."** (Colossians 1:12)

We are the lilies, we are the spices, and we are the honey. Jesus has declared, **"You have ravished My heart My sister, My spouse, you have ravished My heart. Oh My love, you are as beautiful as Tirzah, lovely as Jerusalem."**

However imperfect and insipid our graces seem to ourselves, Jesus finds in them a sweet savor. To His sensitive nature there is a fine aroma in our lowliness and patience, in our love and praise, which we had not thought of ourselves. In our fresh passionate love, in our simple zeal, and in our childlike trust, Jesus finds the profoundest satisfaction.

The sweetest songs of angels do not touch His heart so much as the first whisperings of a penitent's prayer. The nearer we get to Jesus the richer joy we experience. There is a rare delicacy in the gladness easier felt than described. It is a feeling, pure, holy, and joyous. It can in its depths leave us breathless. He has gone to the beds of spices where deep-rooted love is blossoming and bearing fruit.

Let me remind you again of the purpose of this look into Song of Solomon so that we keep our focus.

<u>It is about intimacy. The words, the expressions, the poetic beauty of the Song of Solomon are meant to lead us into a spiritual place where we can experience intimacy with our Bridegroom, our lover.</u>

"Eat O' friends, and drink. Drink deeply, O' lovers."

Just as a refresher, whom is the Song of Solomon referring to when speaking of the Bridegroom and the bride? The Bridegroom refers to Jesus and the bride refers to those who believe that Jesus is the Son-of-God, that He forgave all their sins at His crucifixion, and rose from the dead to restore their relationship to the Father God. As the <u>Bible</u> declared in John 1:12, **"To all who receive Him, He**

gives the right to become children of God. All they need to do is trust Him to save them."

Song of Solomon is a love letter from Jesus to His bride. But it is also a love letter to those who do not know Jesus personally. So like the Daughters of Jerusalem, they can desire Him and cry, **"Where has your Beloved gone that we may seek Him with you."**

We still see the blemishes on our gown, the mud splatters, but our Beloved looks past that and views us as His bride without spot or wrinkle. We need to see ourselves that way also. And that is what Song of Solomon is about – the passion Jesus has for His bride, and for those He desires to enter into the bridal relationship with Him.

There is a beautiful song titled "Before the Throne of God Above." Some of the lines state it very clearly, "Because the sinless Savior died, my sinful soul is counted free, for God, the Just, is satisfied to look on Him and pardon me." My name is graven on His hands, my name is written on His heart.

So let's sit at Jesus' feet, or cuddle up on His lap if you wish, and listen as He describes how beautiful we are. Yes, Jesus desires this intimacy. In John 13:23 as the disciples had their last meal with Jesus, John says of himself, **"Now there was leaning on Jesus bosom one of His disciples, whom Jesus loved."**

Verse 4 – **"O my love, you are as beautiful as Tirzah, lovely as Jerusalem. Awesome as an army with banners."**

Tirzah and Jerusalem at that time were two of the most beautiful cities in the world. Tirzah means delight. Scripture uses the symbology of cities in reference to the people of God. Jerusalem is said to be the perfection of beauty. Psalm 48 speaks of

Jerusalem, **"Great is the Lord and greatly to be praised in the city of our God, in His holy mountain. Beautiful in elevation, the joy of the whole earth."** The New Jerusalem described in the book, Revelation, is called the bride of the Lamb.

We have to understand that this is the poetic language of the East, but as we are looking for an impartation from the Lord, I trust that the Holy Spirit will bypass our western logic and impart its true essence to us.

The beauty of the bride is overwhelming, it is subduing. It is all conquering like an army with flying banners going forth to victory. As the scripture says, "awesome as an army with banners." This is a strange way to describe one's beauty. Almost like somehow this statement was inserted here by mistake. But taken in a spiritual sense it is saying that the church, the bride of Christ, in the presence and power of the Lord is irresistible.

So the purity and excellence of the church will delight the Lord, and no power shall be able to stand before it. Wickedness must flee before righteousness as a defeated host before a victorious army. This is difficult to understand so let's view it from a different angle.

The bride is beautiful not only for her attractive gentleness; she has an authoritative quality, a queenly dignity. The beauty of the church is a severe beauty like the martial beauty of a bannered army. Have you ever watched a good parade with bands and banners? There is a feeling akin to the sight of beauty that rises up in you. It is another dimension of the beauty of the bride.

The Bridegroom is so taken with affection for His bride, (you and I), that He uses many comparisons to describe her. Now we have to understand that He is looking at her in a spiritual sense as well as physical. In fact we could say that it is not physical at all. He looks at us, His bride, as His redeemed creation, perfect in every way. The one for whom His heart beats. But the Lord uses physical descriptions to represent what His heart feels.

Verse 5--**"Turn your eyes away from Me for they have overcome Me. Your hair is like a flock of goats going down from Gilead."** This is the same description given in Chapter 4:1. We looked at these Eastern pictures presented there as a whole panorama, and allowed our spirits to drink in the fragrance, peace,and beauty of it all. Now we need to handle the loveliness of Chapter 6 the same way.

The goats in that region are mostly black or dark brown, while the sheep are white. From a distance the goats upon the lush mountainside present a lovely view, and especially among the romantic scenery of Gilead.

Most of us have not had the opportunity to view such a scene, but we have seen in the green freshness of spring a lovely pasture with cows and their young contentedly grazing. It is one of those scenes that poets and artists try to capture.

Verse 6,7 – **"Your teeth are like a flock of sheep which have come up from the washing. Everyone bears twins, and none among them is barren "Like a piece of pomegranate are your temples behind your veil."** A reasonable interpretation regarding these verses is given in Chapter 4, Verses 2 and 3.

If the entire Song of Solomon were to be summarized in just one statement it would be Verse 5. **"Turn your eyes away from Me, for they have overcome Me."**

If the love, affection, and passion of Jesus for you could be expressed in one statement it would be, **"Turn your eyes away from Me, for they have overcome Me."**

PRAYER
Precious Jesus, how great is Your passion for me, how infinite is Your love. It is overwhelming. I ask You to bring me to that place where I can say to You, "Turn Your eyes away from me, for they have overcome me."

Verse 8, 9 – **"There are sixty queens and eighty concubines and virgins without number. My dove My perfect one is the only one, the only one of her mother, the favorite of the one who bore her. The Daughters saw her and called her blessed, the queens and the concubines, and they praised her."**

Again, this is oriental, poetic language. We can't improve on it. We can't dissect it or rewrite it without destroying its essence.

In those times there were harems and the king selected only the loveliest virgins for the harem. Here the Bridegroom is stating that His bride's beauty is far above all the queens and concubines. That she is her mothers dearest one, and pure one, that she is the perfect one, the darling of her mother. She is the Bridegroom's dove, His undefiled one, and she stands alone in His affections, no others come even close.

She is the bride. You are the bride. These declarations are about you.

As we saw in previous praises from the Daughters of Jerusalem, so good was she and so lovely in character as well as in person that even those who might be expected to be envious call her blessed.

Verse 10 – **"Who is she who looks forth as the morning, fair as the moon, clear as the sun and awesome as an army with banners**."

"Who is she?" This question occurs three times in Song of Solomon. It is an expression of admiration. It is like our seeing a beautiful woman or supremely handsome man coming toward us. In our colloquial manner of expression we would probably say, "Wow, who is that."

Now the maiden's meet the bride after an interval, and are startled by her surpassing beauty, grace and majesty. Her happy love with her Bridegroom has covered her with a new grace. She is clothed in queenly attire. She is a vision of rare loveliness.

It is the love of Christ, which gives the church whatever beauty it possesses. Christ's love for her, drawing forth her responsive love for Him, gives her whatever grace she may have. All that she is and all that she has comes only from His gift. Her appearance is like the early dawn, coming forth in its beauty, coloring sky and clouds with rosy light. She is clear and pure as the sun. As seen in Verse 4, there is a component of supreme beauty that is awesome. Awesome, majestic, stirring as an army marching with banners.

Verse 11 – **"I went down to the garden of nuts to see the abundance of the valley, to see whether the vine had budded and the pomegranates had bloomed."**

As the maidens praised her beauty and stateliness she reminds them of her former low estate. Remember she was a country maiden. She seems to be looking back to the hour of her first meeting with the Bridegroom. As a country maiden she had no thought of the elevation that awaited her. She had gone down into the garden to tend it and to watch the budding of the fruit trees. It was there that she first saw the King.

Until He calls us we are like the bride in Song of Solomon immersed in worldly pursuits and earthly care. We had no thought of the elevation that awaited us.

Verse 12 – **"I knew not"**, she says, **"My soul made me as the chariots of my people, a princely people."**

So now the bride has been raised to a lofty position, and is awe-inspiring in her majesty, like a bannered host, or the chariots of a princely people. Her soul, she says, had made her this. She means her soul's love for the Bridegroom, whom she so often describes as, **"Him who my soul loveth."**

She takes pleasure in looking back upon bygone days, and calling to mind the remarkable manner in which, through the King's admiration and favor, she was raised from a lowly state to the highest position among the ladies of the land. This illustrates the change, which takes place in the experience of the soul that has been visited by the mercy of God in Christ Jesus. It has been raised from a state of pitiable depression and hopelessness to participation in the life and fellowship of the Son of God.

Verse 13 – **"Return, return, O Shulamite. Return, return, that we may look upon you."** The bride had retired. The Beloved and His friends eagerly call her back, **"Return, return."** They desire to look again upon her beauty.

CHAPTER 7

This is another expression of the bride's beauty, and her queenly grace. Remember in Chapter 6, the bride's beauty, her desirability, grace, and nobility are so overwhelming that the Beloved must beg her, **"Turn your eyes away from Me for I am overcome with your perfection."**

Be reminded again that these are the thoughts of the Bridegroom, Jesus, for the bride, each of us. Now something that must be added here is that, yes this is the expression to the church, the body of Christ as a whole, but it is also an expression to each of us as individuals.

This is a vital distinction that we have to understand. We don't just happen to be a part of a large assembly that Jesus adores and so we kind of join in with it. No, we join in with it because we are an individual person for whom Jesus has great passion. We must get this in the correct perspective.

Now as in other parts of this love song, this is treated in the Oriental fashion, so we have difficulty understanding the terminology. I will try to draw forth some of the sense of the individual references to help us get hold of the infinite and intimate passion of our Lord for us individually. Do not expect to find symbolic meaning for all the details in the descriptions. The general intention is to set forth the beauty and glory of the bride.

Please don't get caught up in "Westernizing" this and trying to rationalize it. It is Oriental. Just allow the intimacy to flood your soul. Not with the head, with the heart. And please bear with me if you are squeamish. I didn't write it, God did.

So, let's look at this King's eulogy of His most precious bride.

It begins with a eulogy to her dancing in verse 1, **"How beautiful are your feet in sandals, O prince's daughter. The curves of your thighs are like jewels, the work of the hands of a skillful workman."**

This description, which is perfectly chaste, is intended to bring before our eyes the lithe and beautiful movements of an elegant dancer. The bandings of the body, full of activity and grace, are compared to the swinging to and fro of jeweled ornaments made into chains.

The description passes from the thighs to the middle part of the body, because in the mode of dancing that prevailed in the East, and probably still does, the breast and the body are raised, and the outlines of the form appear through the clothing, which is of light texture. **"Thy navel is like a rounded goblet, wherein no mingled wine is wanting; your waist is like a heap of wheat set about with lilies."** In Syria the color of wheat is considered to be the most beautiful color for the human body. Even today the appearance of heaps of wheat, which are seen in long parallel rows on the threshing floors of a village, is very pleasant to a peasant, and the comparison in Song of Solomon every Arabian will regard as beautiful. The lilies are enhancements. We cannot expect to find a symbol for all the details of these descriptions. As said before, the only intention is to set forth the beauty and glory of the bride of Christ. There is nothing indelicate in these pictures, though it is scarcely Western.

Let's take a little side journey here.

Referring to King Jesus, Psalm 45 says, **"God your God has anointed You with the oil of gladness more than Your companions. All your garments are scented with myrrh and**

aloes, and cassia out of the ivory palaces by which they have made You glad."

Now it refers to the bride, **"King's daughters are among Your honorable women. At your right hand stands the queen in gold from Ophir. The royal daughter is all-glorious within the palace. Her clothing is woven with gold. She shall be brought to the King in robes of many colors."**

Revelation 19:7,8-Referring to the return of Jesus the Bridegroom says, **"Let us be glad and rejoice and give Him glory for the marriage of the Lamb has come, and His wife has made herself ready. And to her it is granted to be arrayed in fine linen, clean and bright, for the fine linen is the righteous acts of the saints."**

We know that when she appears as a bride adorned for her husband it is not the outward adorning but the hidden person of the heart. Now God has clothed us with the fine linen, with the robe of righteousness. **"As many as have been baptized into Christ have put on Christ."**(Galatians 3:27). Jesus is our righteousness.

Now if we mar or stain our robes, as we often do by carelessness and sin, we can come to our Bridegroom in humble penitence and confession asking Him to wash our robes and make them white again in His blood, because it cleanses us from all sin as Psalm 51:7 assures us, "**Purge me with hyssop and I shall be clean. Wash me and I shall be whiter than snow."**

Verse 2- **"Your navel is a rounded goblet which lacks no blended beverage?"**

The "rounded goblet" with mixed wine (wine mixed with water or snow) is intended to convey the idea of the shape of the lovely body with its flesh color appearing through the semi-transparent clothing, and moving gracefully like the diluted wine in the glass goblet.

Verse 3 – **"Your two breasts are like two fawns, twins of a gazelle."** Refer to chapter 4:5 for details on this.

Verse 4 – **"Your neck is like an ivory tower, your eyes like the pools in Heshbon by the gate of Bath Rabbim. Your nose is like the tower of Lebanon which looks toward Damascus."** In Chapter 4:4 her neck is compared to the tower of David.

We can almost visualize an ivory tower. We have seen towers in this country that are built simply for architectural grace and beauty. In Solomon's time there were many towers of architectural and artistic splendor.

Not only is her neck compared to a tower, but her nose as well.

If we were to compose poetry about a lovely bride, how would we phrase it, to what would we compare her neck and her nose? Why compare at all? Why not just say, your neck is lovely, stately, and your nose also. This is not poetry, not love language, and comparison should be made as one thing to another for which a reputation has already been established.

In the Song of Solomon the tower referenced is not just any common tower. It is an ivory tower, the tower of Lebanon. This particular tower was probably well known, covered with ivory tablets, perfect in structure, dazzlingly white in appearance, imposing and captivating.

Her nose forming a straight line down from the forehead would convey the impression of symmetry, and at the same time dignity and majesty.

Referring back to Chapter 4:4 further majesty is added to the tower. **"Your neck is like the tower of David built for an armory on which hang a thousand small shields. All shields of mighty men."**

Why reference to the shields and armory. In Chapter 6:10 she is compared to an awesome army with banners. The mighty men were awesome, heroic, and highly respected. Their shields were of bronze. A thousand gleaming bronze shields hanging on a dazzling white tower would indeed be awesome and resplendent.

Verses 4 and 5 continue with her praises. **"Your eyes are like the pools in Heshbon by the gate of Bath Rabbim. Your head crowns you like mount Carmel, and the hair of your head is like purple. The king is held captive by its tresses."**

In a dry land there is no greater pleasure than to look upon cool, clear, sparkling water. The comparison could also mean that her eyes glistened like the surface of a clear pool.

"Your hair is like purple," describes, at least in one sense, that the intense blackness of her hair casts a purple hue as the tresses catch the light. As the Bridegroom beholds His bride in all of her perfect and varied features of beauty, as she moves gracefully in the dance He is filled with delight and admiration. He is **"held captive in her tresses."**

It is difficult when we try to describe something to another, to help them understand a heart feeling, an inner grasp of a spiritual nature, as we know it. Poets do this. We only have words, spoken or written to convey what we are trying to get across. During the spoken word emotions will help to convey our meaning.

We use the example of an orange. To someone who has never tasted an orange you cannot describe it. You must taste it for yourself.

The phrases, comparisons, descriptions used here in Song of Solomon are to peel away the skin from the orange so that we can take a taste of the sweetness of the fruit. Then we will know.

Psalm 34:8 – **"Taste and see that the Lord is good."**

And what is our theme? **"Eat O friends and drink. Drink deeply O' beloved ones."**

Verses 6-9 – These verses can be considered as a conversation between the two lovers, the bride and the Bridegroom. Now the Bridegroom (Jesus) begins with a general assertion of the delightfulness of His beloved, then in like manner of the Greek poet Theocritus compared Helen to the straight Cyprus tree, here the Bridegroom likens the bride to the tall, straight palm; the loveliest of all trees in his eyes. Man's sister, as the Arabs call it.

"How fair and how pleasant you are, O love with your delights. This stature of yours is like a palm tree, and your breast like its clusters. I said, I will go up to the palm tree; I will take hold of its branches. Let now your breasts be like clusters of the vine, the fragrance of your breath like apples, and the roof of your mouth like the best wine."

Verse 9 can be understood as an expression of the Bridegroom's desire that His bride's mouth may be like the best wine gliding over His lips and teeth.

More on the palm tree:

The palm tree is exalted in Psalm 92, **"The righteous shall flourish like the palm tree."** Several characteristics make the palm tree an apt emblem of the faithful servant of God. There is its tall and graceful appearance, its evergreen foliage, its fruitfulness, and especially the fact that both fronds and fruit grow at the topmost height of the tree, high above the earth and as near as possible to heaven.

Smith's dictionary of the Bible makes the statement, "Well is the life of the righteous likened to a palm, in that the palm below is rough to the touch, and enveloped by dry bark, but above it is adorned with fruit fair even to the eye. Below it is compressed by the enfolding of its bark; above, it is spread out in amplitude of beautiful greenness." For so is the life of the elect, despised below, beautiful above.

The palm tree is also a symbol of the cross. But this just speaks further of the infinite love of the Bridegroom, Jesus, to give Himself for His bride.

The Bridegroom compares His bride to the palm tree and to the vine. Both are fair to look upon. Both have sacred associations. In John 15:5 Jesus declares, **"I am the vine, you are the branches."**

"I will go up to the palm tree; I will take hold of its branches." The bride could have spoken these words, or at least she may have interrupted him and transferred this description as applying to him rather than herself. Certainly the palm tree resembles the Bridegroom in its stateliness and beauty. This view would also lend itself to spiritual applications. The palm tree to Christians represents the cross.

Also where the Bridegroom says, **"The fragrance of your breath is as the fragrance of the choicest fruit, and the tone of your**

voice sweet as the best wine." Here again the bride interrupts, adding the words, **"That goes down smoothly for my Beloved."**

Each seeks to please the other, to exalt the other, put the other first. There is a mutual love that binds them together. She knows how with a confident and happy knowledge that her heart is His. Perhaps as we saw in Chapter 2:16 and 6:3 there had been a little coyness, some hesitation, some doubts, but now there is none. She has given her heart and she knows it.

In Chapter 2:6 she spoke, **"My Beloved is mine and I am His."** Here in verse 10, she goes deeper from her heart, **"I am my Beloved's and His desire is toward me."**

O' how blessed is the soul that can say from the depths of the heart, "I am my Beloved's and He is mine." As the psalmist declared, **"Whom have I in heaven but Thee, there is none upon the earth that I desire beside Thee."** She is as sure that His heart is hers as that hers is His.

The Bridegroom loves the church. His desire is toward His people. Their salvation was the joy set before Him for which He endured the cross.

"I am my Beloved's and His desire is toward me, His heart is set on fire toward me."

Through this revelation we find freedom from striving to attain a certain spiritual level to convince God to love and enjoy us. We can truly and deeply know that God passionately enjoys us. He adores and desires us, even as we struggle to mature and grow in Him. Something awakens inside of us when we know what God is like.

We were created by God to resonate with Him. We come alive and are invigorated when we come in contact with the extraordinary knowledge of the uncreated God who enjoys us, desires us, and has paid the ransom for us.
I Corinthians 2:9,10 – **"Eye has not seen, nor ear heard, nor have entered into the heart of man, the things which God has prepared for those who love him. But God has revealed them to us through His Spirit."**

David understood that God is a fountain of passionate spiritual desire, and shared that with us in Psalm 36:8,9. **"We are abundantly satisfied with the fullness of Your house, and You give us drink from the river of Your pleasures. For with You is the fountain of life. In Your light we see light."**

In Psalm 16:11 David further articulates the theology of God's pleasure for His people that burns in His heart, and the pleasure that He imparts to His people in His embrace. **"You will show me the path of life; in Your presence is fullness of joy. At Your right hand are pleasures for evermore."**

Luke 12:32 – **"Fear not little flock for it is your Father's pleasure, joy, desire, delight, and passion to give you the Kingdom."**

The beauty Jesus possesses is the very beauty that He imparts to His bride in the gift of righteousness. Where does deep lasting, superior pleasure comes from? Very simply it comes from the throne of God, from God himself. It is found in God's burning desire and passion for us.

God is so much different than the way we have customarily thought of Him. Until we can begin to desire intimacy with Him it is extremely difficult if not impossible for us to understand that He longs for us, to be one with us, to have one heartbeat with us. This higher dimension of spiritual intimacy is called "union with God." It is in union with God that we find the greatest exhilaration, and it is also where we discover the most glorious enticements to explore the cavernous depths of God's burning heart.

And to repeat again during this seeking in Song of Solomon, union with God, intimacy with God is where we are headed. Jesus is an affectionate Bridegroom overcome with passion for His bride.

Isaiah 49: 15, 16 – **"Can a woman forget her nursing child and not have compassion on the babe of her womb? Yes, she may forget. But I will not forget you. See I have inscribed your name on the palms of My hands."**

Verse 11-13 – **"Come my Beloved, let us go forth to the field, let us lodge in the villages. Let us get up early to the vineyards, let us see if the vine has budded, whether the grape blossoms are open and the pomegranates are in bloom. There I will give You my love. The mandrakes give off a fragrance, and at our gates are pleasant fruits, all manner new and old which I have laid up for you my Beloved."**

In Chapter 4:8, **"Come with Me from Lebanon My spouse, with Me from Lebanon."** The King had invited His bride to His royal city of the time of their espousal. Now in the following verses she is inviting the King to visit with her to her old home, the scene of her labors in the vineyards.

"Come my Beloved, she says, let us go forth into the field." So as the heavenly Bridegroom calls to Himself the souls whom He so dearly loves, the bride in answer to the Lord's gracious invitation responds by her own invitation, **"Come my Beloved."**

Man was made, not for solitude, but for society. Not for selfishness but for love. The soul, which yields itself to Christ, delights in His fellowship and finds therein its true satisfaction. Like the bride here is saying to her Spouse **"Come, my Beloved, let us go forth into the field,"** the soul craves the society of the Savior and longs for His perpetual companionship.

But the most delightful fields will not satisfy unless the Beloved is there. Could we say that our own soul is the vineyard? Christ's presence will make the vine flourish, and the tender grapes appear. The fruit of the Spirit is love, joy, peace, long-suffering, gentleness, faith, meekness, and temperance. The fruit of righteousness which is ours through Jesus. The fruit is all from Him, as the master gardener, therefore it is fit that it should be all for Him.

When the bride invites the King to revisit the home of her childhood and the scenes of their earlier acquaintance and attachment, among other alluring representations she assures Him that there will be found laid up for His use by her thoughtful affection, all manner of precious fruits, new and old. Are not these fruits which in this earthly life Christ's people are expected to prepare for Him at His coming, and which it will be their delight to offer to Him as the expression of their grateful love. Are we not to grow precious fruits for the approval and service of the Lord?

Why are they laid up for Christ? They are the fruit of His own garden, the growth that testifies to the care and culture of the Divine Husbandman. They will yield a peculiar satisfaction and pleasure to Him the Bridegroom.

Ah, but how sweet it is to the bride. Think of when you gave a special gift to a very special person. Was not your joy and excitement overflowing?

How can we wait, how can we bear the wait until the time we can be in our Bridegroom's presence, face to face, and share His joy as we hand Him our gifts of love. As the bride declared, **"Come my Beloved, let us go to the vineyard, there I will give You my love."**

CHAPTER 8

In Verses 1 and 2, the bride continues her address.

"Oh, that You were like my brother, who nursed at my mother's breasts. If I should find You outside, I would kiss You and I would not be despised. I would lead You and bring You into the house of my mother, she who used to instruct me. I would cause You to drink of spiced wine of the juice of the pomegranate."

Yes, how lovely this is. She is still speaking to the King, telling Him of her love. Remember He had again and again called her His sister. **"My sister My spouse."**

She now wishes that He were to her as a brother that they could have been children of the same mother, that they could have known one another from infancy. So in the close union of lovers there is a longing and desire that they could have known each other from the beginning. That instead of the years in which they were strangers, and never heard one another's voice, or touched one another's hand, they had always been together, and known one another through and through in all the varied experiences of child-life, of girlhood and boyhood.

The bride wishes that she had always thus known the Bridegroom; that she could have loved Him always with a sisterly affection; that their mutual endearments might have been like those of brothers and sisters without shame, attracting no observation. Some in the world may despise her intimacy with the Bridegroom where they would not if they were brother and sister.

How often do we long with an intense longing that we had always from the beginning known and loved our heavenly Bridegroom. How utterly wasted and lost those years now seem which were spent without that knowledge of Christ which is eternal life. How strongly we wish that they could be blotted out of our remembrances with all the ignorance and all the sin. As we draw closer to our Bridegroom, our Lover, we long that we had always remembered Him; that we had kept our hearts pure from other loves, and had always loved Him.

We love Him because He first loved us. As we relate to the bride here, how can we express our love to our beautiful Savior, our Bridegroom and Lover? As we look back to the last verses of Chapter 7, she invited her lover to enjoy the fruit of the garden. She offers Him the spiced wine and delicious juice of her pomegranate. The wine, pomegranate juice, and her kisses are certain expressions of her love.

Now love would want to give to the Beloved. The kisses, the spiced wine, the pomegranate juice that the bride offers to her Lover suggest to us that our Bridegroom desires our affection. **"Let Me see you, let Me hear your voice, for your voice is sweet and your countenance is lovely."**

Jesus is inviting us into a deep, intimate, romantic fellowship with Him.

When the disciples were gathered in the upper room to fellowship in what we call the Last Supper, there was a very touching, poignant, affectionate moment between Jesus and John as we read in John 13:23. **"Now there was leaning on Jesus bosom one of His disciples whom Jesus loved.**

We can't just read this as a statement of an event. As we have been learning to do with the Song of Solomon, we have to visualize this, place yourself there, even put ourselves in John's place. To just touch the hem of His garment would be almost too much emotion to endure. To take His hand would send unendurable thrills of delight running through us. But to lay your head on His breast, to hear His heartbeat for you, to feel His warmth, to experience the security of His strength, to be washed in the love flowing from His being, is far beyond description with words.

Even Jesus cannot endure the infinite depth of the love He feels for His bride. Remember in Chapter 6; he said, **"Turn your eyes away from Me, for they have overcome Me."**

The Jewish custom was for the bride and Bridegroom to become betrothed. That is more than an engagement. They are promised to each other, and then the formal wedding ceremony comes. This is where we are, and there is going to be a wedding. I mean a wedding like no one can imagine. This is going to be a heavenly wedding. And I believe that Jesus is going to dance with each one of His brides individually. And there is going to be joy unspeakable throughout the halls of heaven. I remember the words from a beautiful song, "Oh how we danced on the night we were wed, we vowed our true love though a word was'nt said."

All of creation will join in. **"For you shall go out with joy, and be led out with peace. The mountains and the hills shall break forth into singing before you, and all the trees of the field shall clap their hands."** Isaiah 55:12.

We can draw from the passionate, glowing language of these words in Song of Solomon an overpowering desire for intimacy, for the closest fellowship, and for endearing friendship.

If you are not yet at the intimacy level where you can bathe His feet with your tears and wipe them with your hair, anoint His head with precious ointment, you can offer Him the sincere affection of your heart. He longs for you. As the bride in Song of Solomon developed in her affection for her lover, so you also will move into that special place, the secret place, precious intimacy with your lover, Jesus.

<u>Remember, Song of Solomon is Jesus' love letter to you to woo you into that place of intimacy.</u>

Let's declare our love for our Beloved Lord again with the song:

I love you Lord
And I lift my voice
To worship You, Oh my soul rejoice

Take joy my King in what You hear
Let it be a sweet, sweet sound in Your ear

Verse 3 – **"His left hand is under my head and His right hand embraces me."** These words are also expressed in Chapter 2:6. There we said that perhaps it would be better rendered as a prayer. Another way to see it is, His left hand under my head to support me when I seem ready to fall, His right hand embracing me to shield me from all evil, to assure me of His love.

Psalm 63:8 supports this. **"My soul clings to You. Your right hand upholds me."**

Verse 4 –**" I charge you O daughters of Jerusalem, do not stir up nor awaken love until it pleases."**

This charge was given also in Chapter 2:7. It is worthy of a repeat explanation here.

The love between the Bridegroom and the bride is true and pure. It is sacred and tender, hence the use of gazelles or does that are gentle, timid creatures. The bride longs for the Bridegroom's love, but the Daughters of Jerusalem must not try to excite it. It is more delicate, more maidenly to wait until love pleases to stir itself, until it springs up spontaneously in the heart of the Beloved.

The relations of the soul with Christ are very sacred. They may be mentioned only to the like-minded and even then only with certain awe and reserve. And there are some communions of the heart with the heavenly Bridegroom which may be divulged to none, not even to the nearest and dearest.

We must wait patiently for the Bridegroom. This is one of our most difficult times for it is for a time we cannot see Him or discern the tokens of His love. We must wait for His good time.

It is a sacred thing. The Daughters of Jerusalem were to listen in silence. They were not to praise or to blame. They were not to stimulate or increase the love of bride or Bridegroom. They were to leave it to its free and spontaneous growth in the heart. It is not to be much talked of. It is to be treasured in the heart. It is that inmost spring of that life which is hidden with Christ in God. It must not be stirred by irreverent talk or disclosure, but it must rest unseen, "until it please," until the right time shall come for speaking of its blessedness.

Verse 5 – **"Who is this coming up from the wilderness leaning upon her Beloved. I awakened you under the apple tree; there your mother brought you forth. There she who bore you brought you forth."**

This is a chorus perhaps from the Daughters of Jerusalem enquiring about who this happy bride may be. And the

Bridegroom points to the apple tree where He had once found her asleep, and to the place where she was born.

Before the Beloved came to her the bride was living in the wilderness. The desert in Arabia is called the "empty corridor." It is barren. Nothing there can satisfy. There you are exposed to human foes, to wild beasts and fierce serpents. Is this not a memory of our own lives before we met our beloved Bridegroom?

The bride is able to come up from the wilderness because she is leaning upon her Beloved. Having given herself into His keeping, she knows that she is safe, that He will lead her aright, that He will never leave her and never forsake her; that if she stumbles she will not be allowed to fall; that if she is faint and weary He will uphold her tottering steps; that if she is fearful; His words and His smile will banish her fears and restore her peace.

We lean upon Jesus because He is our well Beloved.

Verses 6,7 – These verses give us a pictorial revelation of Jesus as the all-consuming Fire of God, the passionate Lover who consumes my soul with His burning love. The longing heart of the bride is expressed here in this beautiful passage.

"Set me as a seal upon Your heart, as a seal upon Your arm; for love is as strong as death, jealousy as severe as the grave; the flames are flames of fire, a most fierce flame. Many waters cannot quench love, nor can the floods drown it. If a man would give for love all the wealth of his house it would be utterly despised."

Is this not our heart cry, whether we know it or not, to love and be loved with this kind of fervency. But in order to give ourselves in unrestrained passion we must know that there is someone who is worthy to be trusted with that level of commitment.

In Luke 24:13-32, After all of the, apparently tragic, events surrounding the trial, death, and resurrection of Jesus, the tomb where He was laid was found to be empty. In utter confusion and despair two of His followers started to walk to Emanus and they talked of all the things that had happened. And as they reasoned about these events, Jesus himself drew near and walked with them, but their eyes were restrained so they did not know Him.

And Jesus questioned as to their conversation and why they were so sad. They then explained the whole sequence of events to Jesus expressing their wonderment at what it all meant. If the tomb was empty, where was Jesus? Jesus replied to them, **"O foolish ones and slow of heart to believe in all that the prophets have spoken. Ought not the Christ to have suffered these things and to enter into His glory."**

As the three entered the village they urged Him to stay with them. And as they sat to eat, Jesus took bread, blessed and broke it, and gave it to them. Then their eyes were opened and they knew Him, and He vanished from their sight. And they said to one another, **"Did not our hearts burn within us while He talked with us on the road and while He opened the Scriptures to us."**

Just as Jesus came alongside these two disciples, His understanding, passion and compassion is revealed to us in a functional, practical way. We sometimes, maybe often, stand in the place of these two, confused, at a loss to understand the ways of God. Then He comes to us just as He did to them and speaks to our heart of the truth of His life, His love, and His purpose. In those moments our hearts are ignited, we see things more clearly, and declare along with those two: **"Did not our hearts burn within us while He talked with us on the road."**

Jesus came to them and He comes to us because He has set us like a seal upon His own heart, and because the fire of His love burns with a violent flame, stronger than death, more powerful than the grave. Like the Shulamite, we long for His touch.

This passage in Verses 6 and 7 reveals that God will implant His own love and jealousy within us that is as strong as death. And nothing can escape its grasp if we yield our hearts to it. When we yield to the love of God, in time no sin or weakness can escape its grasp in the same way that nothing can escape the grasp of death in the natural realm. It does not matter how much our hearts have been bitter or angry, or to what degree we have sinned. The Lord can chase down such things. In the same way that death conquers everything in the natural, God's love conquers our hearts and overcomes sin that lives in our hearts. He can chase down the areas of our hearts that seem so prone to stray.

It's with His fire of love that the Lord seals our hearts unto His own. We love Him with the supernatural power of His own imparted love. We love Him because He first loved us. The icy waters of sin, bondage, and persecution cannot extinguish this supernatural fire of God's love when we yield to its all-consuming power.

"If a man would give for love all the wealth of his house, it would be utterly despised."

If one has given up everything they have accumulated they will despise the notion that it was somehow a noble act. They acted because they were totally preoccupied with the love for another. Next to such love, money has no value. In Philippians 3:8 Paul said he considered his sacrifice, the loss of all things, as rubbish compared to the excellency of experiencing the beauty of Jesus.

When we are so preoccupied with the love and beauty of Jesus, the power to respond in wholehearted love toward God is the only reward we want. The power to love is our great reward.

We were made for the exhilaration of passion and will search for the reality of that exalted place. But it is only in the presence of Jesus that the longing is fulfilled.

PRAYER
Thank You Jesus for revealing yourself. Thank You for making my heart burn with passion to know You, to see Your glory. I love You, my Beloved, and by Your sure grace I will follow You all of my days and enter into a limitless intimacy with You.

Verses 8,9 – **"We have a little sister, and she has no breasts. What shall we do for our sister in the day when she is spoken for? If she is a wall, we will build upon her a battlement of silver. And if she is a door, we will enclose her with boards of cedar."** Literally, **"If she be a wall,"** probably refers to steadfastness in virtue, the door referring to the opposite character. These statements are interpreted with much difficulty, but in keeping with our purpose I believe the following is accurate.

It seems to be an inquiry on the part of those who we heard speaking in verse 5 who we said were the Daughters of Jerusalem. They must have known the story of the bride who was now returning with her Beloved, **"Who is this coming up from the wilderness leaning upon her Beloved?"** This question even shows a bit of surprise. But then they listen to her entreaty addressed to her Beloved, **"Set me as a seal upon Your heart, and a seal upon Your arm."**

They then present the question in Verses 8 and 9 concerning a younger sister of the bride, who is not yet of marriageable age. If she were a wall, firm and steadfast, she will be richly dowered; but if she were a door, too easily opened, too accessible, she must be carefully guarded. **"What shall we do for her?"** She must be enclosed with sacred restraints as with boards of cedar. We can spiritualize these statements for our instruction and benefit as telling of the concern for others, which the redeemed soul cherishes. In John 4, when the Samaritan woman at the well found Christ, she sought that others should find Him too.

What must be said here is that when we as the bride of Christ become filled with the unfathomable love of Christ, that love will not, cannot, remain pooled within us. It overflows its banks and becomes a river of love. "What shall be done for her." We also cannot allow our little sisters and brothers to miss our wonderful Bridegroom.

By now we have come to the place where the overwhelming love of our precious bridegroom has brought us into an intimacy with Him where we can say "Oh Jesus, how I long to dance with You, how I long to wash Your feet with my tears and dry them with my hair; to walk hand in hand with You in our garden where at your sweetness even the birds hush their singing, where I can say, "Kiss me with the kisses of Your mouth, lead me away and I will run after You."

PRAYER

Father, thank you for bringing us into that place where we can know and experience the width, the length, the height, and the depth of Your passionate love for us.

Verses 10-12 – Here the bride speaks again. **"I am a wall, and my breasts like towers. Then I became in His eyes as one who found peace. Solomon had a vineyard at Baal Hamon. He leased the vineyard to keepers. Everyone was to bring for its fruit a thousand pieces of silver. My own vineyard is before me. You, O Solomon, may have a thousand, and those who keep its fruit two hundred."**

One thing we glean from these verses is that the bride proudly asserts her purity and maturity, and her Beloved honors her as she becomes in His eyes as one who has found her peace in Him. **"He is mine and I am His."** One who finds peace is the same as one who finds favor, one who is the object of His affection.

Esther 2:17 – **"The king loved Esther more than all the others and she obtained grace and favor in his sight more than all the virgins; so he set a royal crown upon her head."** It is the likeness of the Bridegroom within the bride that makes her beautiful.

Perhaps the most fitting way to receive understanding and grace from these Verses 10 and 12 is this interpretation.

The whole spirit of it justifies the view that the Shulamite is speaking of her person. She invites her beloved Bridegroom to rejoice in the beauty and fragrance of her garden, to pluck the fruits, to revel in its delights. Everything that is pleasant and lovely is there. She exclaims, **"My own vineyard is before me."** That is, all of this delight is in my power, and my desire is to my Beloved; all that I have is His. Like the far-famed keepers of Baal-hamon, I will give the King a thousand shekels, that is, the utmost that the vineyard can produce, and those that keep the fruit thereof shall have two hundred. The king shall be satisfied and all those who labor for the King shall be well rewarded.

Herein is the Father glorified in the Son, when those who bear the name of the Beloved bear much fruit. Then the keepers of the vineyard will themselves rejoice not that they reap a harvest of the world's goods but because their hearts are one with Him whose vineyard they keep, and to see the fruit abound is to fill them with joy.

Verse 13 – **"You who dwell in the gardens, the companions listen for your voice. Let me hear it."** These now are the words of the Bridegroom addressed to the bride. She is the dweller in the gardens; the one who is at home in the gardens, the one whose beauty blends with the loveliness around her.

Here we are drawing to a close this most beautiful, touching, inspiring, and sentimental declaration of passionate love of any love letter ever written. We want to say, "No this can't be the finish. If there isn't more then let me go back and read it again and again."

And there is more. The Bridegroom Himself, our lover, will come to us and continue to reveal greater depths of His fiery love.

But look at these words a little closer. It is delightful to Him to hear her voice, and delightful to those who have been accustomed to that voice from childhood. Remember in Chapter 2:14 the Bridegroom entreated her, **"Let Me hear your voice, for your voice is sweet."** "Dear country girl, sing to Me, and let Me revel in the sweetness of your music." This is an exquisite and tender conclusion to the Song of all Songs. In the next verse 14 the bride is heard singing one of the old familiar strains of love with which she poured out her heart in the days when her Beloved came to her in her home. **"Make haste my Beloved, and be like a gazelle or a young stag on the mountains of spices."**

How can we conceive of a more perfect conclusion.

This is a glimpse of the old love songs, which the bride used to sing. She sings them again now at the request of her Bridegroom Himself, and to the delight of her companions. She goes forth leaning on her Beloved to rejoice in the beautiful scenery and rural pleasures with Him whose presence heightens every joy, the life of her life, and the soul of her soul, all her salvation, and all her desire. The love song, with which she first expressed her love, is now lifted up into anticipation of the everlasting hills of fragrant and joyful life.

The fragrant spices from every believers life which have been cultivated on earth, compounded together, will become a veritable mountain of delightful spices that will be presented to the Lord Jesus on the final day.

The fragrance of your life is an aroma that moves the heart of Jesus like nothing else can touch Him.

Yes, come quickly; make haste, Lord Jesus, that we might rejoice upon the mountains of spices.

CONCLUSION

This time of soaking in the intimacy and beauty of Song of Solomon has just opened the door to intimacy with the author, Jesus, the Beautiful One, the Saviour.

God has delivered an invitation through His Son, Jesus, the Bridegroom. **"Now hear this everyone who is thirsty, come to the waters. And you who have no money, come, buy and eat. Yes, come, buy wine and milk without money and without price. Incline your ear and come to Me. Hear, and your soul shall live"** (Isaiah 55:1).

Jesus has promised, in John 6:47, **"Surely, I say to you, he who believes in Me has eternal life."** And in first John 5:11, **" God has given you eternal life and this life is in His Son Jesus Christ."**

And to those who come, you have a new song:

My name is graven on His hands
My name is written on His heart
Because the sinless Saviour died
My sinful soul is counted free
For God, the Just, is satisfied
To look on Him and pardon me
My life is hid with Christ on high
With Christ my Saviour and my God

AMAZING LOVE